Commendat...

For far too long the Ch··
apostolic responsibil
Embracing the Poor is a
the Church in its missio   ...ng
proclamation and practi   .equilibrium.

κev Dr Joel Edwards
Director, Micah Challen,   ...ιional and former General
.rector Evangelical Alliance(UK)

I visited a church recently and the pastor ran through their values; evangelical, authority of the Bible, charismatic, believer's baptism, priesthood of all believers. Then he said something was missing. 'What we need is the DNA of the Salvation Army.' Meaning their heart for the poor. This is not an 'add-on' but something to be developed deep in the DNA of Church. This book is very timely and goes beyond biblical teaching about God's heart for mercy and justice and New Testament Church teachings. It is full of practical advice and stories. It will move you, it will challenge you, it will change you. Be warned.

Geoff Knott
Former Executive Director, Wycliffe Bible Translators

Filled with practical guidance and rich in biblical principles, this excellent work is the fruit of labour in several nations and with diverse cultures. Every church leader and those particularly engaged in working with the poor would hugely benefit from reading it and embracing its principles.

Terry Virgo
Founder and Leader of Newfrontiers

The apostolic priority of caring for the poor and needy is well addressed in this volume which will be of immense value to any church seeking to reveal God's heart in this key area of our witness. It will show the way for many years to come.

John Kpikpi
Newfrontiers Apostolic Leader, Ghana

The mix of powerful biblical teaching with practical case-studies of exemplary action make this book a sling and stone for anyone working in communities where poverty is a giant to be faced.

Scott Marques
Newfrontiers Apostolic Leader, Zimbabwe

I happened to be at the *Newfrontiers* leaders' conference when Simon Pettit threw down the gauntlet to the *Newfrontiers* family of churches to take up the apostolic mandate to care for the poor. This book is the fruit of over ten years' of work in responding to that challenge. The message of the book is piercing and powerful, the thrust inescapable, and the practical guidance offered very helpful. I was captivated. Many of our young people who have a passion for justice and compassion will be too. I will be recommending this book far and wide!

Steve Thomas
Leader, International Apostolic Team, Salt & Light Ministries

Those who want to follow the apostolic mandate to 'remember the poor' will find in this book a series of helpful articles and testimonies from people who have been at the forefront of *Newfrontiers'* efforts to demonstrate the love of God with the gospel in one hand and practical care in the other.

Adrian Warnock
Author, Raised With Christ

Embracing the Poor

Dedication

This book is dedicated to the memory of Simon Pettit who, together with his wife Lindsey, enthusiastically embraced the poor and through his lifestyle and teaching encouraged many others to do likewise.

Embracing the Poor

Commissioning Editor
David Adams

Newfrontiers International

RoperPenberthy Publishing Ltd

Published by RoperPenberthy Publishing Ltd
Springfield House, 23 Oatlands Drive, Weybridge, KT13 9LZ

All Bible quotations are from the New International Version unless
otherwise stated.

First published in 2011

ISBN 978-1-903905-71-5

Cover design by Robin Ireland

Typeset by RoperPenberthy Publishing Ltd

Printed in Sweden by ScandBook AB

Contents

Foreword

Please read this book. In it you'll find answers to burning questions that we should all be asking. The writers explain why caring for the poor and marginalised is absolutely integral to following Jesus, why proclamation and demonstration of the gospel are indivisible. We learn why and how the local church is the indispensable agent of change in bringing sustainable, holistic transformation to those living in poverty. And why our efforts to help the poor must go way beyond simply improving their health and income, to embracing a goal that sees their relationships restored with God and neighbour.

Embracing the Poor is packed with biblically-grounded wisdom, disturbing facts, thoroughly practical advice, inspiring stories of transformation and loads of prophetic vision. It all very definitely inspires us to act.

We journey through scripture – the Law, Prophets, Gospels, Acts and Epistles – and are brought face-to-face with the incontrovertible truth that our God is passionate about people living in poverty. This passion, like a golden thread, runs throughout the Bible. Enshrined in the Law to protect the orphan and widow. Fuelling the uncompromising words of the Prophets as they confronted injustice and oppression. Shaping the compassion and love of Jesus as he identified with the marginalised and downtrodden. And we discover, too, the breathtaking example of the early church that modelled such a radical love of the poor that contemporary writers and even emperors were compelled to take note.

There's a deep authenticity to this book – all that's written is based not only on God's word, but also on the lived experience of numerous local churches across the *Newfrontiers* network. These are local churches that have gone beyond remembering the poor to embracing them wholeheartedly – love in action.

The book is a trumpet call to each of us to embrace God's passion for the poor and to rediscover the early Church's apostolic mandate to care for the least, the lost and the last. We are shown that this call to compassionate action must not be delegated, outsourced or subcontracted. It is for us all. As we each remember the poor we are called to go out – into our communities, into the world – to love these people in word and simple deed, all in the power of the Holy Spirit.

In this way, the writers invite us to reconnect with the example of the early church – a community that radically modelled the life of the Kingdom of God that Jesus proclaimed, in which could be seen the inauguration of the new humanity.

At Tearfund we have placed the local church at the heart of both our vision and all we seek to do to confront poverty and injustice. Because, when it comes to sustainable, holistic, cost-effective transformation of people living in poverty, I believe nothing compares to the effectiveness of the local church – a community of people inspired by the love of God, empowered by the Holy Spirit, to make real that same love to all who are in need.

This is the inspiring and enduring hope that this book expounds.

Matthew Frost
Chief Executive, Tearfund
April 2011

Contributors

Here are some biographical details on the contributors to the main chapters in this book, in the order in which their contributions appear.

David Adams is a South African, born in Port Elizabeth in 1954. Growing up in apartheid South Africa, his faith in Christ encouraged him to believe that personal and social transformation were possible and that God was passionately concerned for the poor and needy and those who were the victims of injustice. A desire to be part of the solution rather than part of the problem sustained him during the 1970s and 1980s, when the situation in South Africa was becoming increasingly polarised. The peaceful transition to democracy that South Africa underwent in the 1990s was experienced as a true miracle, an intervention by God. David's studies at the universities of Rhodes, Cape Town, UNISA and Stellenbosch have been in the humanities, education and theology. After serving with Youth With A Mission in Namibia and South Africa, he spent eleven years in teacher training in Cape Town while serving since 1985 as an elder at Jubilee Community Church. In 1994 David joined the staff team at Jubilee. Through the years this local church has increasingly become a community that embraces people of different races, cultures, languages and nationalities – a community that reflects the diversity of the nation of South Africa, seeking to bring believers together and see them caught up in God's purposes. David's passion is teaching and training people for God's mission. David and his wife, Herma, live in Cape Town and have two grown-up children, Jonathan and Marieke.

Steven Oliver grew up in Cape Town, South Africa where, on the completion of his schooling, he worked and underwent training in the manufacturing industry with a large international group. In 1984 Steven joined a young friend and pioneered a business in the electronic security field for fifteen years; this included the design, manufacture and distribution of in-house products that were later distributed through a network of franchises. In 1994 Steven responded to a prophetic word to go to the 'daisies of Africa and take hope to the hopeless.' He subsequently left Cape Town with his family and moved to the rural area of Clarens in the Free State, where he started working among the poor, bringing the gospel of hope. This resulted in the establishment of a school, the provision of training in farming methods, and many other programmes aimed at poverty alleviation. Following God's call to 'raise people from the ash heap and seat them with princes', Steven has given himself to raising and releasing leaders to impact poorer communities around the world. After fourteen years of work in the central regions of South Africa and Lesotho, he now lives in Dubai, UAE, with his wife, Heather, and continues to serve God, not only among the affluent in this new and modern city, but also among the poor in many nations that they are involved in around the world. Steven and Heather have three sons, Cameron, Richard and Adam.

Martyn Dunsford was born in London in 1952. While studying chemistry at Southampton University in the early 1970s he came to faith in Jesus Christ. After a few years teaching science and physical education in an independent grammar school he pastored two large and growing churches, first in Bradford, West Yorkshire, and then in Southampton. Since 1987 he has been pastor of Kings Community Church, Southampton, which started as a small group of believers that has grown to become the large church it is today. Martyn and his wife Gaynor have a passion for the local church both to serve its local community and reach the nations. They have a heart especially for the poor and disadvantaged. Martyn is founder of Care and Relief for the Young (CRY), a children's charity dedicated to the restoration of destitute young people; CRY has worked in some 40 nations over the years. Martyn is also a founder board member of SEEDFUND UK which provides micro and medium start-up business loans to help the poor become self-sufficient. He is also the international director of the Kings Community Church College, set up to provide quality short-term training for internationals – especially those from poor backgrounds. Martyn himself travels widely initiating and building up churches while prioritising poorer nations. Martyn and his wife, Gaynor, live near Southampton, England. They have three adult children and one grandson.

John Hosier grew up in North London and joined a Baptist church there. On leaving school he spent some time in the merchant navy and in local government before training as a Baptist pastor at Spurgeons College and obtaining a theology degree from London University. He pastored two evangelical Baptist churches before lecturing for some years at Moorlands Bible College, mainly in New Testament Studies. In 1986 he became a full-time elder at Church of Christ the King in Brighton. John led the team for about eight years before engaging in a wider ministry of preaching, lecturing and teaching in the UK and overseas, though still based as an elder in the Brighton Church. Following 'retirement' in 2009 he has spent a year working with Jubilee Community Church in Cape Town and in 2011 joined the leadership team at Citygate Church, Bournemouth. Amongst other writings he has authored the books, *The End Times, The Lamb, the Beast and the Devil: Making Sense of the Book of Revelation,* and *God's Radiant Church,* as well as contributing regularly to Scripture Union Bible Notes. Married to Sue, they have two sons and seven grandchildren.

Nigel Ring read Mechanical Sciences at Cambridge University and Rehabilitation Engineering for a research degree before leading a research team in a paediatric hospital designing artificial limbs and researching other matters related to physical handicap. In 1981 he became full-time Administrator to Terry Virgo, who had already planted a church out of Nigel's home in 1977, as he gathered an apostolic team. Since then Nigel has served Terry personally and the *Newfrontiers* family of churches in an administrative capacity. In 2000 God called him to an added responsibility for helping churches internationally to become more active in serving people who were poor or disadvantaged within their local communities. He had already been involved administratively in his local church (Church of Christ the King, Brighton) with homeless people, those with HIV/AIDS and those who had had unplanned pregnancies. In 2001 he launched Act Together, a five year initiative within *Newfrontiers*. In 2004 he joined an international task team led by Simon Pettit to develop strategy for *Newfrontiers* for ministry among the poor. This was later led by Steven Oliver after Simon's death and is the Team behind the current book, *Embracing the Poor*. Nigel lives with his wife, Janita, in Hove. They have four adult children and two grandchildren.

Alan Norton is an elder at River of Life Westgate Church in Harare, Zimbabwe, having previously led the team of elders for four years. During 2006–2008 he led a team that planted Stapleford Community Church northwest of Harare, and was originally part of the team under Piet Dreyer's leadership who planted the first *Newfrontiers* church in Zimbabwe at Bindura. He is also part of Scott Marques' apostolic team. His passion is establishing churches through training, discipling and equipping leaders for eldership, with special emphasis on remembering the poor. He does this using Foundations for Farming and Foundations for Family as vehicles, while helping leaders to provide sustainably for their families. He has wide experience working with donors and directing ministry projects that are church based and serve rural communities. Recently he has become involved in working alongside Mbonisi Malaba and Sam Poe in using Chronological Bible Storying as a strategy for church planting. Alan and his wife, Deb, live in Harare and have four children.

Preface

The *Newfrontiers* family of churches grew around the apostolic ministry of Terry Virgo who, from 1980, gathered a team of trans-local ministries as described in Ephesians 4:11–13. Key emphases were:

- restoring the Church to a New Testament pattern;
- discipleship;
- training leaders;
- reaching out to the nations evangelistically;
- planting churches on the back of this evangelistic endeavour.

Ministry related to the poor was somewhat peripheral in those early days. However, in 1998, at the *Newfrontiers* International Leaders Conference in Brighton, UK, a clear trumpet call was brought by Simon Pettit, an apostolic leader based in Jubilee Community Church, a *Newfrontiers* church in Cape Town, South Africa. Based on Galatians 2:10 Simon powerfully showed that to 'remember the poor' is an apostolic commission – it is not negotiable. He called the *Newfrontiers* family of churches to lay hold of this distinctly New Testament apostolic emphasis in whatever we do – in apostolic ministry, church planting, evangelism and in all of church life.

In 2003 a significant meeting was held in Germany to consider strategy for the way forward among *Newfrontiers* churches. Out of this meeting various task teams were formed. One, relating to ministry with the poor, was to be led by Simon Pettit. However, before it had gathered momentum, Simon was taken from us through a heart attack while ministering in New Zealand.

It was not until 2006 that Steven Oliver was approached and agreed to a request from Terry Virgo and his team to pick up Simon's mantle in this regard. He was asked to gather a task team with the purpose of devising a strategy that would ensure that the New Testament apostolic injunction to 'remember the poor' would be integrally part of all that *Newfrontiers* was engaged in. Steven began by consulting with various *Newfrontiers* leaders from a number of nations during the course of 2006, and the composition of the task team was consolidated at a significant gathering in February 2007 at Dihlabeng, Steve's home church in Clarens, South Africa. The Dihlabeng church has been intentional in seeking to minister to the poor in a holistic way. It is a church where caring for the needs of the poor is integrally part of preaching the gospel, seeing people saved and added to the church community, seeing their lives transformed in Christ and seeing society impacted for good.

The motivation for gathering the task team came from the desire to take seriously the apostolic and prophetic call that had been sounded loud and clear over the previous decade – a call that had been given particular profile in Simon Pettit's exhortation to 'remember the poor' at the conference in Brighton in 1998.

At that same conference Priscilla Reid – accompanying her husband, Paul, from Belfast in Northern Ireland, as a guest at the conference – prophesied that we need to begin to look at nations and continents, not from a human perspective but from God's perspective. The focus of the prophetic word then turned to the continent of Africa as Priscilla continued:

> *The Africa I am building is an Africa with a golden platter, full of the good things of God, and there is a stream out of Africa to bless the nations of the world. The Africa that I am building has a golden platter in front of it that will never be empty and has the ability not only to feed its own people, but to feed the nations of the world.*

Whereas Africa is so often seen as a continent that holds out an empty begging bowl, God's desire is to turn that around so that the continent will be able to feed itself – materially, spiritually and in every other way. Indeed, God's desire is to go far beyond that and turn Africa into a source of food and provision for the nations of the world. What a breathtaking prophetic word; it gave vivid expression to God's passion to gather the poor and needy to be part of his people, transforming them and catching them up in his purposes in the nations!

Simon Pettit's exhortation and the prophetic stirrings at the Brighton Conference in 1998 provided an impetus to work this through in both our theology and practice as *Newfrontiers* churches in various nations. Thus, for example, at the *Newfrontiers* 'Joy in the City' Conference in South Africa in 1999, David Devenish directed attention to the first few verses from Isaiah 61 as an indication of God's perspective on those who were poor, those who were in captivity, those who were in terrible bondage:

The Spirit of the sovereign Lord is on me, because the Lord has anointed me to preach good news to the poor. He has sent me to bind up the broken-hearted, to proclaim freedom for the captives and release from darkness for the prisoners, to proclaim the year of the Lord's favour… to comfort all who mourn, and provide for those who grieve in Zion – to bestow on them a crown of beauty instead of ashes, the oil of gladness instead of mourning, and a garment of praise instead of a spirit of despair. They will be called oaks of righteousness, a planting of the Lord for the display of his splendour. They will rebuild the ancient ruins and restore the places long devastated; they will renew the ruined cities that have been devastated for generations.
(Is 61:1–4)

David Devenish pointed out that these verses clearly proclaim that God's perspective is neither merely to feed the poor nor simply to preach good news to the poor – though both are integrally part of his intentions. God's perspective is that those who *were* the poor and those who *were* the captives become those who *now* lead in his kingdom purposes.

While some can have an almost patronising attitude to poor and needy people, God's heart is not like that at all. God's heart is to take us when we're dead in our sins and to make us ambassadors for his righteousness. God takes those who are broken, those who are poor, those who are captive, and he makes them instruments of excellence in his kingdom purposes. David Devenish noted that this is precisely what is affirmed here in Isaiah 61. It is the poor, the captives, the needy who will be full of praise instead of despair. It is they who will be called 'oaks of righteousness, a planting of the Lord for the display of his splendour'! Those who were previously the poor and needy will 'rebuild the ancient ruins and restore the places long devastated; they will renew the ruined cities that have been devastated for generations.'

At this same conference in Cape Town both Simon Pettit and David Devenish referred to a prophecy brought by David N'dharuhutse of Rwanda at a similar 'Joy in the City' conference, also in Cape Town, three years earlier. He had spoken of three winds that God would cause to blow from West Africa, East Africa and Southern Africa respectively, that would mingle together and impact the whole continent of Africa, including the North. It was in North Africa, as David Devenish pointed out, that the early Church had flourished dramatically, before being devastated by the spread of Islam in the 7th and 8th centuries. These are ancient ruins that are going to be rebuilt and restored. Surely God is going to use those who were poor and oppressed to rebuild the ancient ruins in places where God once worked in amazing power.

God delights in taking the poor and needy to make them his own, catching them up in his purposes – in his mission! In recent years *Newfrontiers* has become more and more active in regions of the world where there is much poverty and need – such as parts of Africa, Asia and Eastern Europe. In the process there is the increasing realisation that God is raising up people in these nations who will spearhead the advance in taking new ground as a family of churches. Indeed, *embracing the poor* is not in some way a separate component in the mission that God has called us into. Rather, *embracing the poor* is integrally part of God's mission. *Embracing the poor* is for the nations!

How have the churches within the *Newfrontiers* family responded to the injunction brought by Simon in 1998? Nearly twenty years ago, at one of the early Stoneleigh Bible Weeks held in the UK, it was decided to interview people who were working with the poor. Among the key protagonists on that occasion were Piet Dreyer and Angela Kemm. Piet had developed a training base in the old prison in Pietermaritzburg, South Africa; Angela was doing a remarkable work in the townships of Cape Town, South Africa, in the days of apartheid which ultimately resulted in the construction of 650 new homes for shack-dwelling families. There were few other ministries in the *Newfrontiers* family at that stage.

Following Simon Pettit's 'call to arms' in 1998, ministries embracing the poor have burgeoned. During 2000, under the banner 'Act 2000', an initiative in the UK intentionally stimulated 20 ministries across different sectors to help them develop models of good practice. In 2002 another initiative was launched internationally, Act Together, to assist churches develop their ministries among the poor through training and networking. By the summer of 2008 there were over 600 known ministries among the 290 churches who responded to a survey of the 600+ *Newfrontiers* churches internationally, each of these ministries touching, on average, at least two development sectors (e.g. drugs and HIV). A total figure for the whole family could well exceed 1000 ministries.

Ministry embracing the poor is now firmly on the *Newfrontiers* agenda. The 'Kingdom manifesto' of Isaiah 61 requires the transformation of the hearts of the poor to be an integral part of the evidence of the effectual gospel and for their circumstances to be significantly impacted. When new churches are planted they are encouraged to start a relevant ministry from the outset, based on the gifting of their members and the needs of the community. Some of those planting these churches themselves come from a root of poverty, and much of the church planting that now takes place worldwide is in contexts of poverty, necessitating that ministries that embrace the poor are integrally part of the very foundations of the new Church.

David Adams, Cape Town, 2011

Chapter 1

God's heart for the poor

David Adams

'Has not God chosen those who are poor in the eyes of the world to be rich in faith and to inherit the kingdom he promised those who love him?' (Jas 2:5). For the apostle James, the answer to this question was self-evident as he looked around at the members of the young church. Has not God chosen the poor? Of course he has chosen the poor! For God is passionate about the poor.

The testimony of the Scriptures is clear. When God selected a chosen people, he gladly picked poor slaves in Egypt. When God established his Church, many of the members of the early Church were drawn from the ranks of the poor. Indeed, when God became flesh, he chose, for our sakes, to become poor (2 Cor 8:9).

It is with the poor that Jesus humbly identified in his incarnation. Born in a stable, a refugee in Egypt, growing up in remote Galilee, dying on a cross like a common criminal, at every point in his life Jesus rubbed shoulders with the poor. He never had any of the riches of this world. When he crossed the Sea of Galilee, it was in a borrowed boat. When he rode into Jerusalem, it was on a borrowed beast. When he was buried, it was in a borrowed tomb.

Jesus clearly saw his mission as bringing good news to the poor. In fact, it was from the prophet Isaiah that Jesus read the following words in the synagogue at Nazareth to mark the beginning of his public ministry:

> *The Spirit of the Lord is on me,*
> *because he has anointed me*
> *to preach good news to the poor.*
> *He has sent me to proclaim freedom for the prisoners*
> *and recovery of sight for the blind,*
> *to release the oppressed,*
> *to proclaim the year of the Lord's favour.*
> *(Lk 4:18–19)*

Jesus specifically singled out the poor as the ones to whom he brought good news. His mission embraced the poor and the needy, for he came to set the prisoners and the oppressed free, and to heal the blind. Certainly the gospel Jesus proclaimed was for all, but he was particularly concerned that the poor and the needy would realise that this good news was for them. They were the ones to whom Jesus seems to have been especially drawn. In the pages of the New Testament we see that the kinds of people to whom Jesus paid particular attention included a blind beggar, a man with leprosy, a woman with a string of broken marriages and a dishonest tax collector. Among those who impressed Jesus we find a widow who placed her last two coins in the offering, a nameless child and a despised woman whom society had rejected. These were the ones with whom the Messiah engaged, the ones he had his eyes on.

Consequently, when the imprisoned John the Baptist sent his disciples to confirm his identity, Jesus' response comes as no surprise. The mark of his authenticity that Jesus provided them with was that he was caring for the needy and preaching good news to the poor:

'Jesus replied, 'Go back and report to John what you hear and see: The blind receive sight, the lame walk, those who have leprosy are cured, the deaf hear, the dead are raised, and the good news is preached to the poor.'
(Matt 11:4–5)

God is passionate about the poor

The Bible leaves us in no doubt as to God's heart for the poor. Both Old and New Testaments paint a picture of God as one who is merciful and compassionate and who cares passionately about those in misery and distress.

Mercy and compassion are intrinsic to God's nature. When God proclaimed his name to Moses, he declared that he was 'the Lord, the Lord, the compassionate and gracious God, slow to anger, abounding in love and faithfulness' (Ex 34:6). God's compassionate nature is celebrated over and over again in the Psalms (e.g. Ps 86:15; 103:8; 111:4; 145:8; 116:5). He is the 'Father of compassion' (2 Cor 1:3) who 'has compassion on all he has made' (Ps 145:9).

Jesus fully reflected the Father's heart of compassion, for, as he told his disciples, 'anyone who has seen me has seen the Father' (Jn 14:9). Compassion was a hallmark of the life of Jesus. As Jesus travelled throughout the towns and villages and saw the crowds, we are told that 'he had compassion on them, because they were harassed and helpless, like sheep without a shepherd' (Matt 9:36). Wherever he went he opened his arms and his heart to the poor and needy, the sick and the oppressed. In fact, these were the ones he specially invited to join him: 'Come to me, all you who are weary and burdened, and I will give you rest' (Matt 11:28).

Let's look at a few examples from Scripture where God's

heart for the poor and needy is vividly displayed. Psalm 113 is a good place to start.

Psalm 113 is an invitation to all people across the face of the earth, 'from the rising of the sun to the place where it sets', to praise his name, since he 'is exalted over all the nations, his glory above the heavens.' It continues:

> *Who is like the Lord our God,*
> *the One who sits enthroned on high,*
> *who stoops down to look*
> *on the heavens and the earth?*
> *He raises the poor from the dust*
> *and lifts the needy from the ash heap;*
> *he seats them with princes,*
> *with the princes of their people.*
> *He settles the barren woman in her home*
> *as a happy mother of children.*
> *(Ps 113:5–9)*

This is one of those breathtaking passages in Scripture where we have God's transcendent greatness contrasted with his immanence – his nearness and close involvement with his creation. Something gloriously unique is being affirmed about God, which prompts the psalmist to exclaim, 'Who is like the Lord our God?' For the one who reigns on high, exalted above all of creation, looks down upon the heavens and the earth with a heart filled with compassion for the poor and the needy, those who have been discarded on the scrapheaps. But, more than that, he delights in exalting the wretched of the earth. He raises the poor from the dust and the needy from the ash heap, and he seats them with princes! He takes pity on the barren woman and comes to her rescue. That is the kind of God he is. No other god can compare with him. In total contrast to the idolisation of celebrities that we see in our world, it is not primarily the wealthy and the famous with whom God delights to fraternise. Rather, as John Stott[1] points out, 'what is characteristic of him is to champion the poor, to rescue them from their misery, and to transform paupers into princes.'

These sentiments expressed in Psalm 113 are echoed repeatedly in Scripture. That God exalts the poor and needy is celebrated in Hannah's song of praise when after years of childlessness her son Samuel was born. The words Hannah used closely resemble those of Psalm 113 as she rejoiced that:

> *He raises the poor from the dust*
> *and lifts the needy from the ash heap;*
> *he seats them with princes*
> *and has them inherit a throne of honour.*
> *(1 Sam 2:8)*

The same theme is echoed centuries later in Mary's song that she sang after learning that she, and not some prominent celebrity of the day, had been chosen by God to be the mother of the Messiah. She marvels at the notion that God has looked beyond her lowly state and raised her to such prominence, and her thanks and praise overflow as she exclaims:

> *He has performed mighty deeds with his arm;*
> *he has scattered those who are proud in their inmost thoughts.*
> *He has brought down rulers from their thrones*
> *but has lifted up the humble.*
> *He has filled the hungry with good things*
> *but has sent the rich away empty.*
> *(Lk 1:51–52)*

---

[1]John Stott, *Issues Facing Christians Today,* p232

Indeed, in Mary's song it is not only the fact that God exalts the humble that is celebrated, but the notion is upheld that God both lifts up the humble and puts down the proud. Jesus is often quoted as teaching that 'everyone who exalts himself will be humbled, and he who humbles himself will be exalted' (Lk 14:11; 18:14; Matt 23:12). Certainly, this truth was exemplified in his own life. Jesus left the realm of glory and made himself nothing; he became like one of us and humbly served; his obedience took him to the very depths of the cross. 'Therefore God exalted him to the highest place...' (Phil 2:5–11). It is this principle, which pledges the reversal of human fortunes, that especially can bring hope to the poor, as Stott[2] points out.

The overall tenor of Scripture leaves us in no doubt that God's eyes are on the poor and needy. God has a heart that is passionate for the poor, and he seems to delight in turning the standards and values of the world upside down. For, in God's economy, the proud are abased while the humble are exalted; the well-fed are sent away empty while the hungry are filled with good things; powerful rulers are toppled from their thrones, while the powerless and the oppressed are raised up to reign like princes.

Who are the poor?

In answering this question from a Scriptural perspective, John Stott's analysis in his book, *Issues Facing Christians Today*, is particularly insightful. What follows here is indebted to his writing on this topic.

Stott[3] has helpfully classified the cluster of words for poverty that occur more than 200 times in the Old Testament (and derive from six main Hebrew roots) as follows:

- The *indigent poor* – those who lack the basic

[2]John Stott, *Issues Facing Christians Today*, p234
[3]Ibid

necessities of life such as food or clothing or shelter.

- The *oppressed poor* – those who are powerless victims of human injustice or oppressive life circumstances.
- The *humble poor* – those who acknowledge their helplessness and look to God alone for salvation.

Of course, poverty is not only confined to the lack of things material such as food, shelter and health, but may also embrace less tangible aspects of a social and cultural nature such as the experience of community and fulfillment.

The poor are therefore not simply those who fall below a certain level of subsistence. They are those who are powerless to determine their own destiny and meet their own needs on a broader front. They include those who suffer from adverse circumstances: the sick, the physically handicapped, the orphaned and widowed, immigrants, slaves and prisoners. In addition, some categories of people are relatively poor because they may be helpless when compared with others in particular societies: for example, the young and the old, women and those who are single. Yet, whatever the particular category of poverty, the Scriptures reveal that God reaches out to the poor and needy, and makes their cause his own.

1. The indigent poor

The Bible acknowledges that people may be numbered among the indigent poor through various sets of circumstances. For some, their poverty may be due to their own sin – whether laziness, extravagance or gluttony. Proverbs, for example, has much to say about this, addressing laziness (Prov 6:6–11; 24:30–34; 10:4; 19:15; 20:13; 28:19) and drunkenness and gluttony (Prov 23:20–21; 21:17). In some circumstances, both individual and national poverty may be due to the sin of disobeying God. God promised to bless Israel's obedience with fruitful fields and orchards, and to curse their disobedience with barrenness (e.g. Lev 26; Deut 8 & 28; Is 1:19–20).

Generally speaking, however, the Old Testament writers saw 'poverty as an involuntary social evil to be alleviated, not tolerated, and they represented the poor (who included widows, orphans and aliens) as people to be offered assistance, not blamed.'[4] These were people who had suffered some form of calamity, often not of their own making. Therefore God's people were commanded not to harden their hearts against their poor brother or sister, but to be generous in assisting those who could not maintain themselves by freely offering them food and shelter (e.g. Deut 15:7–11).

The Old Testament Law contained numerous provisions aimed at alleviating the plight of the indigent poor. For example, the regular tithes were to be used to support not only the Levites, but also the aliens, orphans and widows in the community (Deut 14:29; 26:12). If an Israelite lent money to someone in need, he was not to charge interest on it (Ex 22:25; Lev 25:36–37). If he took someone's cloak as pledge, he was to return it before sunset because the poor person would need it as a blanket to sleep in (Ex 22:26–27; Deut 24:13). Employers were to pay their workers' wages promptly, the same day that they were earned (Lev 19:13; Deut 24:14–15). And there were detailed provisions to ensure that the indigent could gather food during the harvest. These provisions reserved the borders of the fields, the gleanings after harvesting and the fallen fruit for the poor, the alien, the widow and the orphan, who were also to be allowed to share in the harvest celebrations (Lev 19:9–10; 23:22; Deut 24:19–21). In addition, every third year a tenth of the agricultural produce was to be given to the poor (Deut

[4]John Stott, *Issues Facing Christians Today*, p234

14:28–29; 26:12); and every seventh year fields were to be left to lie fallow, and vineyards and olive groves to be left unharvested, for the benefit of the poor who could help themselves to the pickings (Ex 23:10–11; Lev 25:1–7).

In passages like Deuteronomy 15:1–15, God put in place safeguards to defend his people from both wealth and poverty. Thus, every seven years God's people were expected to release all debts and all slaves; every seven years the balance in the economy would be restored. For, as Terry Virgo[5] has pointed out, God wanted his people to enjoy community as a whole. Therefore, while God blesses industry and hard work, his intention was that neither would the rich get too rich nor would the poor be crushed. In this sense God is more interested in the peace of the community as a whole than any individual concept of 'fairness'. He wants a harmonious, caring community.

The Old Testament wisdom literature also reflected this genuine concern for the poor. In Proverbs 31:20, it is noted that one of the characteristics of a righteous man or woman is that they would be generous and lend freely; whereas, 'if a man shuts his ears to the cry of the poor, he too will cry out and not be answered' (Prov 21:13). Indeed, there is the clear understanding that behind the poor God himself is standing, their Creator and Lord, so that people's attitude to him is reflected in their attitudes to the poor. Consequently, on the one hand, 'he who mocks the poor shows contempt for their Maker' (Prov 17:5); and, on the other hand, 'he who is kind to the poor lends to the Lord' (Prov 19:17).

Jesus himself inherited and built on this rich Old Testament legacy of care and concern for the poor. In the Gospel accounts, we see him making friends with the needy and feeding the hungry. Jesus told his disciples to sell their possessions and give alms to the poor (Lk 12:33), and when

---

[5]In a message entitled, 'They Will Be My People', delivered at the Stoneleigh Bible Week in England in 2001.

giving a party to remember to invite the poor, the crippled, the lame and the blind, who would most probably be in no position to invite them back (Lk 14:12–14). He also assured them that in feeding the hungry, clothing the naked, welcoming the homeless and visiting the sick, they would in fact be ministering to him (Matt 25:35–40).

It is not surprising, therefore, that care for the poor and needy was a central focus in the New Testament Church, as reflected in Acts. Paul devoted considerable attention to the provision of relief aid for the poor Christians in Jerusalem from other Christian communities in the Eastern Mediterranean region, as is evident in several of his letters in the New Testament. And James urged his readers to care for those in need, defining *true religion* in the following terms: 'Religion that God our Father accepts as pure and faultless is this: to look after orphans and widows in their distress and to keep oneself from being polluted by the world' (Jas 1:27). What a telling statement, that caring for orphans and widows is at the very heart of true religion!

2. The oppressed poor

In the Old Testament there is the recognition that people are not simply reduced to poverty without rhyme or reason. Some calamity or other could plunge people into poverty. Personal sin or national disobedience, and God's judgment on them, could result in poverty. However, poverty was often due to the sins of others. A situation of social injustice could easily deteriorate because the poor were not in a position to change it. 'We do not understand the Old Testament teaching on this subject unless we see how frequently poverty and powerlessness were bracketed.'[6]

God is a God of justice and he champions the cause of the powerless and oppressed. Psalm 140:12 proclaims, 'I know

[6]John Stott, *Issues Facing Christians Today*, p236

that the Lord secures justice for the poor and upholds the cause of the needy.' For this reason, the law of Moses laid special emphasis on the need for impartial justice in the courts, in particular for the poor and powerless, warning against perverting justice through bribery (Ex 23:6,8) or showing favouritism to the influential (Lev 19:15). The rationale repeatedly given for upholding justice was that God's people themselves had been oppressed in Egypt, and the Lord had rescued them and set them free (Deut 15:15).

The wisdom books were just as explicit in demanding justice for the powerless. So, for example, in Psalm 82 the judges were instructed to 'defend the cause of the weak and fatherless' and 'maintain the rights of the poor and oppressed' (Ps 82:1–3). In Proverbs 31, King Lemuel was exhorted by his mother to 'speak up for persons who cannot speak for themselves, for the rights of all who are destitute', to 'speak up and judge fairly' and 'defend the rights of the poor and needy' (Prov 31:8–9; cf. Prov 22:22; 29:7,14).

The prophets were forthright in fiercely condemning injustice. They urged God's people to seek justice, encourage the oppressed, defend the cause of the fatherless and plead the cause of the widow (Is 1:17). They forbade them to 'oppress the widow or the fatherless, the alien or the poor' (Zech 7:10). And they frequently spoke out against the rulers of Israel and Judah for exploiting the poor. For example, Elijah rebuked King Ahab for murdering Naboth and stealing his vineyard (1 Ki 21); Amos berated the rulers of Israel who, in return for bribes, trampled on the heads of the poor, crushed the needy and denied justice to the oppressed (Amos 2:6–16; 4:1; 5:11–12; 8:4–6) and Jeremiah denounced King Jehoiakim for using forced labour to build his luxurious palace (Jer 22:13–17).

In speaking out against injustice and exploitation, Isaiah 58 cuts to the heart of the matter. Fasting is a sham in God's eyes if not accompanied by justice. An accusation is brought against the people: 'Yet on the day of your fasting, you do as you please and exploit all your workers' (Is 58:3). The prophet continues to define what true fasting is – fasting that is acceptable to God:

> *Is not this the kind of fasting I have chosen:*
> *to loose the chains of injustice*
> *and untie the cords of the yoke,*
> *to set the oppressed free*
> *and break every yoke?*
> *Is it not to share your food with the hungry*
> *and to provide the poor wanderer with shelter –*
> *when you see the naked, to clothe him,*
> *and not to turn away from your own flesh and blood?*
> *Then your light will break forth like the dawn,*
> *and your healing will quickly appear;*
> *then your righteousness will go before you,*
> *and the glory of the Lord will be your rear guard.*
> *(Is 58:6–8)*

From the Old Testament prophetic writings it is readily apparent that the Lord's passion for justice was a two-edged sword. When the people of God were oppressed, it led to their freedom. But when they became the oppressors, it led to their destruction – as witnessed in the captivity and the exile in Babylon.

In the midst of the frequent failure to uphold justice for the powerless in the kingdoms of Israel and Judah, the prophets looked expectantly to the coming Messiah's righteous reign. They longed for his coming, for, 'with righteousness he will judge the needy, with justice he will give decisions for the poor of the earth' (Is 11:4).

This concern for justice for the powerless and oppressed

is also reflected in the New Testament. James, for example, condemned the wealthy specifically for the fraudulent withholding of wages from their workforce and their violent oppression of the innocent (Jas 5:1–6).

Clearly, 'the biblical writers saw the poor not only as destitute people, whose condition was to be relieved, but also as the victims of social injustice, whose cause should be championed.'[7] God calls his people to be the voice of the voiceless and the defender of the defenceless.

3. The humble poor

The humble poor are those who are spiritually meek and dependent on God. They are the 'poor in spirit' (Matt 5:3), who readily receive the gospel. They are those who are aware of their personal poverty and their helplessness to liberate themselves; they know that they are in need of a rescuer, and may just be driven to put their trust in God. They may look to him for mercy. Zephaniah describes them as 'the meek and the humble, who trust in the name of the Lord' (Zeph 3:12), and Isaiah calls them the 'humble and contrite in spirit' (Is 66:2). They are not so self-sufficient as to imagine that they can draw close to God on the basis of what they have to offer. Indeed, the dependence and receptivity of the poor is a biblical paradigm for receiving salvation and entering the Kingdom of God. The confidence and self-sufficiency of the wealthy, on the other hand, often precludes them from humbly receiving salvation.

The Psalms are, in a sense, the hymnbook of the humble poor, for they are filled with humble expressions of dependence on God, and they recall God's promises to come to the aid of the helpless. These are 'the lonely and afflicted' who cry to God to be gracious to them (Ps 25:16). They are the ones who commit their way to the Lord, who are quiet

[7]John Stott, *Issues Facing Christians Today*, p237

before him (Ps 37:5, 7) and wait patiently for him to act (Ps 40:1). They are given assurance that 'the poor will eat and be satisfied' (Ps 22:26), that 'the meek will inherit the land' (Ps 37:11), and that the Lord 'crowns the humble with salvation' (Ps 149:4). And the Psalms include some inspiring individual testimonies to the Lord's salvation (Ps 34; 86).[8]

Jesus proclaimed, 'Blessed are the poor in spirit, for theirs is the kingdom of heaven' (Matt 5:3). In essence, Jesus was saying, 'Blessed are the desperate!' A person who is poor in spirit, or mourning, or persecuted, or hungry and thirsty for righteousness has a peculiar advantage over the rest. For, with nowhere else to turn, the desperate may just turn to Jesus, the only one who can offer the deliverance they long for. As Philip Yancey says, 'Human beings do not readily admit desperation. When they do, the kingdom of heaven draws near.'[9] The humble poor, or the 'poor in spirit', are those:

> *who acknowledge their bankruptcy before God. They have no righteousness to offer, no merit to plead, no power to save themselves. They know that the only way to enter God's Kingdom is to humble themselves like little children and receive it as a gift. So they come as beggars, with nothing in their hands.*[10]

The humble poor are not self-reliant or self-sufficient. They do not trust in their own strength and abilities, but recognise their deep need of God. To such Jesus says, 'Theirs is the kingdom of heaven' (Matt 5:3). By contrast, the rich or self-satisfied, who imagine they have something to offer rather than that they are in need, are sent away empty-handed.

With John Stott's help, we have distinguished between

---

[8]John Stott, *Issues Facing Christians Today*, p238
[9]Philip Yancey, *The Jesus I Never Knew*, p117
[10]John Stott, *Issues Facing Christians Today*, p238

the indigent poor, the powerless and oppressed poor and the humble poor. While the Bible challenges indolence, the Scriptures view the poverty of the indigent and the oppressed as a social evil which God opposes. However, there's a poverty of the spirit in which God delights, and this is discernible in the 'humble poor'. In Stott's words, God:

> *succours the indigent poor, champions the powerless poor and exalts the humble poor. In each case 'he raises the poor from the dust', whether it be the dust of penury or of oppression or of helplessness.*[11]

Is God on the side of the poor?

If God is passionate about the poor, does that mean that he is on the side of the poor? Some speak of God's *bias*, or *preference for*, or *solidarity with* the poor. Is such language appropriate? Certainly, as we have already noted, the Scriptures frequently teach that God exalts the humble and abases the proud. But does this mean that God sets his face against all those who are wealthy or powerful, and that God actually sides with the poor? In attempting to answer this question, it is important to remember a few things.

First, God is not biased. 'There is no favouritism with him' (Eph 6:9). In fact, Scripture explicitly forbids partiality (Lev 19:15; Deut 1:17; 16:19; 1 Tim 5:21; Jas 2:1). Thus, God does not care more about the salvation of the poor than of the rich.

Second, material poverty is not a biblical ideal. Indeed, the Scriptures point out the dangers of poverty; for poverty isolates people from family and friends (Prov 14:20; 19:4,5), and poverty puts people at the mercy of the rich and powerful (Prov 18:23). Rather, the Scriptures uphold the

[11]John Stott, *Issues Facing Christians Today*, p237

ideal that there should be no poor in the land (Deut 15:4). In reality the Bible counsels that it is better for people to be neither rich nor poor, but to have enough and be content (Prov 30:8).

Third, being poor and oppressed does not in itself make people members of the church. The poor need to repent and be saved by God's justifying grace just as much as the wealthy.

While teaching that God is not biased against the wealthy per se, the Bible does however affirm that he casts down the wealthy and powerful when they become wealthy by oppressing the poor (Prov 22:16,22–23), or even when they fail to share with the needy (Prov 21:13). Interestingly, in the story of the rich man and Lazarus in Luke 16, Jesus does not say that the rich man exploited Lazarus; he merely points to his lack of concern for the sick beggar lying outside his gate.[12] Consequently, as Randy Alcorn says, 'ignoring the poor is not an option for the godly'.[13]

God is concerned about justice, and so, while God shows no partiality, he is also not neutral in situations of injustice. Specifically because God is not biased in pursuing justice, God favours the poor who are either victims of injustice or find themselves in a position in which they are powerless to resist the oppression of the powerful. In that sense, God is on the side of the poor. He has a special concern for them because of their vulnerability. It may be helpful to draw an analogy: parents love their children equally, but when one child is ill, the parents will demonstrate a particular concern for that one. The God of the Bible is on the side of the poor precisely because he is a God of impartial justice who cares about everyone.

It is helpful to understand that God does not distinguish between people in the way that society so often does. Indeed,

[12]Ronald Sider, *Rich Christians in an Age of Hunger,* p53
[13]Randy Alcorn, *Money, Possessions and Eternity,* p230

in this respect God appears to delight in overturning the values of society in pursuing his mission:

> *God has chosen to change the world through the lowly, the unassuming, the imperceptible – his people. God chose a ragged bunch of Semite slaves to become the insurgents of his new order. He sent a vast army to flight with 300 men carrying lamps and blowing horns. He chose an undersized shepherd boy with a slingshot to lead his chosen people. And he worked through a baby in a stable to turn the world right side up!*[14]

God delights in taking the lowly, the marginalised and the seemingly insignificant, and redeeming them, giving their lives significance as they are woven into his magnificent purposes. As Paul reminds us, 'God chose the foolish things of the world to shame the wise; God chose the weak things of the world to shame the strong. He chose the lowly things of this world and the despised things – and the things that are not – to nullify the things that are, so that no one may boast before him' (1 Cor 1:27–29). In this sense, God is on the side of the poor.

What about the poor outside the community of faith?

Does God care about the poor and needy who are not numbered among the community of faith? And does this have implications for God's people?

The Scriptures declare that God rules over all creation and all people:

> *The Lord has established his throne in heaven,*
> *and his kingdom rules over all*
> *(Ps 103:19).*

[14]CRUDAN, *Christian Wholistic Development*, p89

The earth is the Lord's, and everything in it,
the world, and all who live in it
(Ps 24:1).

As Creator and Redeemer, God cares about the total well-being – both spiritual and material – of all the human beings he has made. Having created them in his own image, he longs that they will discover their true humanness in their relationships to him and to one another. Therefore God yearns after his creatures in their lostness, and calls on them to heed his word, repent and receive his forgiveness, that they might truly be his people. But, at the same time God cares for the poor and the hungry, the alien, the widow and the orphan, he denounces oppression and tyranny, and calls for justice; and he instructs his people to be the voice of the voiceless and the defender of the powerless, and so to express their love for them.[15] It is neither an accident nor a surprise, therefore, that Jesus should sum up all the Law and the Prophets in the two great commandments that we are to love God with all our being and our neighbour as ourselves (Matt 22:37–40). And, in defining the word 'neighbour', Jesus told the story of the Good Samaritan – someone who was clearly regarded as an outsider by the Jewish community (Lk 10:27–37).

Therefore, while God clearly intends that the poor within the community of faith are cared for, the Scriptures show that God cares also for the poor and needy in general. Consequently it is God's intention that his people would also care for the poor and needy wherever they are encountered. This is evidenced in the concern for the alien or stranger that is a significant focus both in the Old Testament and in the teaching and example of Jesus. It also fits with the kind of 'Kingdom perspective' that the Bible advocates.

[15]John Stott, *Issues Facing Christians Today*, p343

Concern for the alien in the Old Testament

While treasuring a very special relationship with his covenant people, it was God's concern to bless all the nations on earth. This concern is visible, for example, in God's commission to Jonah to go and preach to the people of the city of Nineveh, and is readily discernible in the breathtaking prophecies of men like Isaiah. But perhaps one of the most tangible displays of God's remarkable care for those outside his covenant people is witnessed in the numerous Old Testament instructions to his people to care for the alien or sojourner in their midst – those who dwelt among the people of God, yet were not part of God's covenant community.

Since Israel occupied a central position in the Ancient Near East, the rise and fall of nations and empires on occasion displaced whole communities and brought refugees to seek shelter among the Israelites. Consequently the number of aliens in their midst was at times quite considerable, as may be seen in Solomon's census (2 Chron 2:17). In such circumstances God wanted his people to be in no doubt that he loved and cared for the well-being of such people, who were frequently listed alongside the fatherless and widows as being defenceless and in particular need of being treated with justice. Indeed, God himself would be their defence and would judge their oppressor. There are numerous Old Testament examples of this, like Deuteronomy 27:19; Psalm 146:9; Jeremiah 7:5–7; 22:3; Zechariah 7:9–10; and Malachi 3:5, to mention just a few. And special provisions ensured that the alien, along with others in special situations of need, would be cared for when harvesting crops or tithing, as seen for example in Leviticus 19:10; 23:22 and in Deuteronomy 14:28–29; 24:14–15,19–21; 26:12–13.

Alongside these instructions, there is the oft repeated refrain that the Israelites, whom God had delivered from slavery in Egypt, should respond with mercy and justice towards aliens in their own midst, since they knew what it was like to have been oppressed as aliens in a foreign land (e.g. Ex 22:21; Deut 24:17–18). Indeed, in the same chapter where the famous and often quoted 'Love your neighbour as yourself' (Lev 19:18) appears, God commands his people to love the alien:

When an alien lives with you in your land, do not
mistreat him. The alien living with you must be treated
as one of your native-born. Love him as yourself, for you were
aliens in Egypt. I am the Lord your God.
(Lev 19:33–34)

The teaching and example of Jesus in caring for the stranger

Building on this strong Old Testament tradition of care for the alien or stranger, Jesus too showed a concern for such people both in his teaching and by example. In the parable of the sheep and the goats, Jesus included the stranger along with the hungry and thirsty, the homeless and the naked, the sick and those in prison, and equated caring for these with serving the Lord himself (Matt 25:34–36,40). In the parable of the Good Samaritan, Jesus intentionally challenged the national pride of the people of Israel and their exclusiveness by commending the actions of a despised Samaritan who disregarded society's barriers to provide care for one of a different ethnic and religious background (Lk 10:25–37). In fact, Jesus went yet further and taught that we are to love even our enemies (Lk 6:27–36).

Practically, while Jesus ministered primarily within the Jewish world, he certainly did not limit his ministry to Jews. Needy people from many varied backgrounds were ministered to by Jesus – Samaritans, Greeks and Romans are all mentioned in the Gospels as recipients of his ministry. At a time when the Pharisees and teachers of the Law were meticulous in trying to separate themselves from any who could be considered 'unclean', Jesus was accused of being 'a friend of tax collectors and 'sinners'' (Matt 11:19) because of the way he reached out to those on the periphery of Jewish society. Unlike the parochial and inward-looking Pharisees, Jesus knew that God's purposes were not limited to Israel. He understood that the 'gospel of the kingdom will be preached in the whole world as a testimony to all nations, and then the end will come' (Matt 24:14). And in the words of the Great Commission that he left with his disciples, Jesus urged them to look outward: 'Go and make disciples of all nations...' (Matt 28:19).

A Kingdom perspective

In essence, the Scriptures exhort us to have a Kingdom perspective when it comes to relating to God's creation and to society at large, since God rules over all creation. The Kingdom was a central focus of Jesus' teaching – a Kingdom characterised by the righteousness and justice of God. Such a Kingdom perspective challenges the church to engage in both evangelism and social ministry, reaching out to those outside its membership, as directed and empowered by the Holy Spirit. And, the church's efforts are invigorated by the profound realisation that, although at this present time there are those who do not acknowledge his rule, a time is coming when all things in heaven and on earth will be brought together under one head, Jesus Christ (Eph 1:10).

Grasping this eschatological truth should go a long way towards freeing us from any 'batten down the hatches' type of mentality. It empowers the believer to engage confidently with society knowing that God's Kingdom is advancing and will indeed ultimately win the day. In his 'Sermon on the Mount', Jesus taught that his followers are not to withdraw but are called to be salt and light in society.

You are the salt of the earth... You are the light of the world...
Let your light shine before men, that they may see your good
deeds and praise your Father in heaven.
(Matt 5:13,14,16)

In an interview published in *Newfrontiers* Magazine, John Stott[16] pointed to the salt and light metaphors in Matthew 5 as a powerful motivation for Christians to permeate non-Christian society. These metaphors dramatically point out that God's people are as different from the world as light from darkness or salt from decay. However, as Stott noted, 'salt does no good if it stays in the salt shaker; it has to penetrate. Light does no good if you hide it under a bed, or under a bucket. It has to penetrate the darkness.' God's intention is that Christians would permeate society and transform it for the good. Putting salt on fish or meat prevents bacterial decay. Turning on a light dispels darkness. Both salt and light transform their environment.

Embracing a Kingdom perspective translates into a willingness to engage with society on many different fronts, upholding God's justice and mercy, and serving the poor and needy, as well as preaching the good news of the Gospel. The Church needs to resist a secularising trend that seeks to confine the Church merely to caring for the spiritual welfare of its members. A strong, vibrant church can be an influence

[16]*Newfrontiers* Magazine *(vol 3, issue 2, Jan–Mar 2007)*, p47

for the common good in society – a gift of God for the freedom and welfare of all people.

Conclusion

God is passionate about the poor. His concern for the poor and for justice is integral to his very nature. Consequently, the church's willingness to care for the poor and needy displays God's passion for the poor. It is love in action.

God's heart is for the poor, and he delights in embracing people who come from situations of poverty and need, to shape them and mould them to play significant roles in his unfolding purposes. In fact, it is good to remember that all who are in Christ are in reality drawn from the ranks of the 'poor'. For, it is a humble recognition of our 'poverty' without Christ and a dependence on God's gracious gift of salvation that is the prerequisite for entry into his Kingdom. 'Blessed are the poor in spirit, for theirs is the kingdom of heaven' (Matt 5:3).

Chapter 2

The New Testament Church's response to poverty

David Adams

Poverty and disease were widespread in Jesus' day. Begging was for some a way of life. Corruption and oppression were endemic. The gulf between rich and poor, freeman and slave, was vast. Wealth was concentrated in the hands of a small elite who gained much of their wealth by exploiting slave labour. The vast majority could expect little more from life than abject poverty.

Indeed, the ancient Mediterranean was an unforgiving place, with little protection from periods of hunger and acute economic and political oppression. Life expectancy at birth was probably between twenty and thirty years. Free workers, skilled or unskilled, lived in constant fear of unemployment. Indeed, beggars filled the cities of the Mediterranean world, and, to a population in which nearly all lived only a little above subsistence level, the beggar embodied their deepest fears.[17] The labourer earned a wage of a denarius a day, out of which he would need to feed, clothe and house himself and his family. Yet, the living costs of a single adult were about half a denarius a day, which gives some idea of the problems faced by larger families. In

[17]Justin Meggitt, *Paul, Poverty and Survival*, p58

times of plenty all who were able-bodied could expect to subsist. But in times of shortage living conditions quickly deteriorated. In such times individuals might be tempted to sell themselves or their children into slavery. For those who were not able-bodied, all times were times of shortage and hardship.

It was these indigent and oppressed poor whom Jesus carried in his heart. These were the ones with whom he identified, with whom he made friends and whom he served. It is no surprise therefore that, when Jesus sent his disciples out to minister in his name, he sent them out in a manner that would make them poor, relatively speaking, in comparison to those whom they would serve (Lk 10:3–4). Those who were to receive the message of God had to recognise that it was being preached by poor disciples, and was for those who were prepared to receive from poor and humble people. Jesus described the cost of discipleship in terms of embracing homelessness (Matt 8:20–22).

It was into such a world that the Church was born. And the early Church rapidly impacted entire towns, cities and regions, drawing many of the poor into this new, alternate community. Consequently, working apostolically among the poor was normal in the context of the New Testament Church. Let us look now in more detail at the response to poverty of this new community that formed around Jesus and became the New Testament Church.

Jesus' new community

The Old Testament prophets had not only warned that Israel would be destroyed because of her idolatry and oppression of the poor; they had also proclaimed a message of hope – the hope of a future messianic kingdom, when God would raise up a righteous branch from the Davidic line. Peace, righteousness and justice would then abound in a new, redeemed community. Writing of this Messiah, this 'Branch from Jesse' that would bear such fruit, Isaiah said: 'With righteousness he will judge the needy, with justice he will give decisions for the poor of the earth' (Is 11:4).

The Old Testament expectation of the Kingdom of God therefore centred on God's promise of a coming ideal King, who would both judge the poor with justice and give the blessing of his rule to the humble and lowly. In the opening chapters of the New Testament Gospels we meet such people – Zechariah and Elizabeth, Joseph and Mary, Simeon and Anna were humble, poor believers. They were looking and waiting for the Kingdom of God, in which God would throw down the mighty from their thrones and exalt the humble and meek.

The essence of the good news that Jesus proclaimed was that the expected messianic kingdom had come (Matt 4:23; 24:14; Mk 1:14–15; Lk 4:43; 16:16). However, the kingdom that Jesus heralded disappointed popular Jewish expectations, for he did not recruit an army to drive out the Romans; nor did he establish a free Jewish state. Without pomp or ceremony, he travelled the country, both preaching the Kingdom and caring for the poor and needy in very practical ways, such as healing the sick, restoring sight to the blind and feeding the hungry. He called and trained disciples, and he established a visible community of followers joined together by their submission to him as their teacher, their master, their Lord. And this new community began to live out Jesus' teachings – the values of the promised Kingdom – which radically transformed the way they related to one another and to those outside the community. This extended, for example, even to sharing a common purse (Jn 12:6) – a practice that included not only Jesus and the twelve, but also a number of women whom

Jesus had healed and who travelled with Jesus and the disciples, sharing their financial resources with them (Lk 8:1–3; Mk 15:40–41).

Jesus' invitation to come and follow him was an invitation to join such a community. Sider[18] points to Jesus' words as illustrative of this new community:

'I tell you the truth,' Jesus replied, 'no one who has left home or brothers or sisters or mother or father or children or fields for me and the gospel will fail to receive a hundred times as much in this present age (homes, brothers, sisters, mothers, children and fields – and with them, persecutions) and in the age to come, eternal life.'
(Mk 10:29–30)

Sider[19] goes on to suggest that these words need to be understood in the context of what was happening among Jesus' followers:

Jesus had begun a new community, a new social order, a new kingdom of faithful followers who were experiencing redeemed economic relationships. The common purse of Jesus' disciples symbolized their amazing availability to each other. In that kind of community, there would be genuine economic security. Each person would indeed have many more loving brothers and sisters than before. The economic resources available in difficult times would in fact be compounded a hundredfold and more. The resources of the entire community of obedient disciples would be available to anyone in need. Such unprecedented unselfishness would certainly challenge surrounding society so pointedly that many would want to join while others, out of jealousy, would want to destroy through persecution. But even in the most desperate days, the promise would not be empty.

[18]Ronald Sider, *Rich Christians in an Age of Hunger,* p78
[19]*Ibid,* p78

Even if persecution led to death, children of martyred parents would receive new mothers and fathers in the community of believers.

This new community that had formed around Jesus was radically transformed by his death and resurrection and the subsequent outpouring of the Holy Spirit at Pentecost; and this provided the foundation for the church that we encounter in Acts.

The Jerusalem church in Acts

The early Church fully embraced Jesus' heart for the poor, and the glimpses that are gained from Acts are breathtakingly inspirational. Immediately after reporting the three thousand conversions at Pentecost, it is noted that 'all who believed were together and had all things in common' (Acts 2:44). Whenever anyone was in need, they shared. Giving surplus to needy brothers and sisters was not enough. They regularly dipped into capital reserves and sold property to aid the needy. For example, Barnabas sold a field he owned (Acts 4:36–37).

Long before, God had promised Israel that obedience would eliminate poverty among his people (Deut 15:4). That promise came true in the earliest Church:

There were no needy persons among them. For from time to time those who owned lands or houses sold them, brought the money from the sales and put it at the apostles' feet, and it was distributed to anyone as he had need.
(Acts 4:34–35)

They were not isolated individuals struggling alone to follow Jesus. A new community, in which all areas of life were being transformed and in which resources were being shared, became a joyful reality. The unusual quality of their shared life together gave power to the apostolic preaching. And this had a phenomenal evangelistic impact, for 'the Lord added to their number daily those who were being saved' (Acts 2:47).

Care for the poor and needy was thus integrally present in the very foundations of the apostolic church. In Acts 6 we see that the apostles themselves were involved in a daily distribution of food, serving the most marginalised – the widows. Clearly this was by no means regarded as a peripheral activity, and it dramatically reflects what was in the apostles' hearts: they were both passionate about preaching the word and about caring for the needy.

This ethos also had an amazing impact on how they worked out problems, as seen in Acts 6, where the injustice of overlooking the needs of the Greek-speaking widows in the Jerusalem church surfaced. The church's response was startlingly counter-cultural. The seven men chosen to look after the matter would appear all to have been from the minority group – for every one of their names is Greek.[20] In effect the church turned over its funds for needy widows to the minority group that had been discriminated against. What was the result of this new kind of financial fellowship? We are told:

So the word of God spread. The number of disciples in Jerusalem increased rapidly, and a large number of priests became obedient to the faith.
(Acts 6:7)

The breathtaking glimpse of the early Church that we have in Acts may perhaps be descriptive rather than prescriptive,

[20]Ronald Sider, *Rich Christians in an Age of Hunger,* p80

but it certainly is challenging. In the midst of the amazing sense of community, caring and sharing that we see here, it is important to note that the church in Acts did not insist on absolute economic equality. Nor did they abolish private property. For example, Peter reminded Ananias that he had been under no obligation either to sell his property or to donate the proceeds to the church (Acts 5:4). Sharing was voluntary, and not compulsory. But love for brothers and sisters was so overwhelming that many freely abandoned legitimate claims to private possessions. 'No one claimed that any of his possessions was his own, but they shared everything they had' (Acts 4:32). That does not mean that everyone donated everything, for later in Acts we read that John Mark's mother, Mary, still owned her own house (Acts 12:12), and other passages indicate that others retained some private property. But, certainly a very different attitude towards possessions was in evidence. When there was need, believers sold lands and houses to aid the needy. 'The needs of the sister and brother, not legal property rights or future financial security, were the deciding factors. For the earliest Christians, oneness in Christ meant sweeping liability for and availability to the other members of Christ's body.'[21]

The apostolic burden for the poor

From the New Testament writings it is abundantly clear that the early apostolic leaders carried a burden for the poor and needy. For example, James urged his readers to care for those in need, defining true religion in the following terms:

> *Religion that God our Father accepts as pure and faultless is this: to look after orphans and widows in their distress and to keep oneself from being polluted by the world.*
> *(Jas 1:27)*

[21]Ronald Sider, *Rich Christians in an Age of Hunger,* p81

In the New Testament epistles there are numerous references to the generous sharing of resources, especially with regard to providing relief for those in poverty. John makes it clear that such sharing of material resources is a hallmark of one in whom the love of God dwells:

If anyone has material possessions, and sees his brother in need, but has no pity on him, how can the love of God be in him?
(1 Jn 3:17)

Paul held the care for the poor very close to his heart. Indeed, he regarded the poor and needy as indispensable in the church community. For Paul rejoiced in the understanding that the Church Jesus is building is characterised by unity in the midst of rich diversity. He likened the Church to a body that is made up of many different parts which are all intended to function together harmoniously for the benefit of the whole (Rom 12:4; 1 Cor 12:12–27; Eph 4:3–16). No part of this body can adopt the attitude that it does not need the other parts: 'The eye cannot say to the hand, "I don't need you!" And the head cannot say to the feet, "I don't need you!" (1 Cor 12:21). In fact, Paul went on to argue that, 'on the contrary, those parts of the body that seem to be weaker are indispensable' (1 Cor 12:22). In essence, Paul was calling the church in Corinth to take special care of the poor and needy among them because they were indispensable, as Stephen van Rhyn[22] has pointed out; without the poor and needy among them, there would in reality be a question mark over their authenticity as a genuine local expression of the body of Christ.

Paul's concern for the poor is reflected in the fact that he devoted a great deal of time to raising funds for Jewish

[22]As Stephen van Rhyn pointed out in a seminar entitled, 'Compassionate, Courageous Leadership', which he delivered at the *Newfrontiers* Leaders' Conference in Brighton, England in July 2009.

Christians in Jerusalem among predominantly Gentile congregations elsewhere. In doing so he ensured the growth and development of intra-church assistance (within one local church) into inter-church sharing across ethnic and geographic lines among the scattered congregations of believers.

When famine struck in AD 46, Paul and Barnabas took economic assistance from Antioch to Jerusalem (Acts 11:29–30). The significance of this act is all the greater when we realise that this represented the first instance recorded in the New Testament of anyone being sent out on an apostolic mission – and the purpose was to provide relief to the poor in Judea. Indeed, Paul's desire to assist the poor Jerusalem Christians materially became a major concern of his apostolic ministry. This is reflected in several of his letters as he arranged for gifts (e.g. Gal 2:10; Rom 15:22–28; 1 Cor 16:1–4; 2 Cor 8–9).

While Paul clearly had others, like Titus, assisting him with the administration of the provision of relief aid to the Judean Christians from the churches in Macedonia, Achaia and elsewhere, without any doubt he himself shouldered an apostolic burden for the poor. He motivated people towards this goal in his teaching and writing. He helped them strategise by setting in place a process for giving, and he involved others to ensure accountability and to safeguard against any charge of embezzlement, as we see for example in 1 Corinthians 16:1–4. Furthermore, he insisted on accompanying the offering personally to Jerusalem, even when he faced personal danger from angry Jews in Jerusalem. For Paul had a deep conviction that this financial symbol of Christian unity mattered far more even than his own life (Acts 21:13).

Why was Paul so concerned with the financial problems of the Jerusalem church? Sider[23] suggests that it was his

---

[23]Ronald Sider, *Rich Christians in an Age of Hunger*, p84

understanding of Christian fellowship, for the word *koinonia* played a significant role in Paul's theology, and was central in his discussion of the collection of the funds for the Jerusalem church. For Paul, *koinonia* or fellowship with Christ involved *koinonia* with all the members of the body of Christ (1 Cor 10:16–17). As Ephesians 2 and Galatians 3:28 teach, Christ's death for Jew and Gentile, male and female, slave and free, had broken down all ethnic, gender and cultural dividing walls. In Christ there is one new humanity, one new body of believers:

> *Consequently, you are no longer foreigners and aliens,*
> *but fellow citizens with God's people and members of God's*
> *household, built on the foundation of the apostles and*
> *prophets, with Christ Jesus himself as the chief cornerstone.*
> *In him the whole building is joined together and rises*
> *to become a holy temple in the Lord. And in him you too*
> *are being built together to become a dwelling in which*
> *God lives by his Spirit.*
> *(Eph 2:19–22)*

Paul used the same word *koinonia* to designate financial sharing among believers. Early in Paul's ministry, after a dramatic debate, the Jerusalem leaders had endorsed his mission to the Gentiles. When they extended 'the right hand of fellowship' *(koinonia)*, they stipulated a single tangible expression of that fellowship: 'Remember the poor' (Gal 2:9–10). This was something that Paul was eager to do. Indeed, it is highly significant to note how care for the poor is clearly taken for granted in this passage (Gal 2:1–10), which deals with a momentous watershed in the early church – the issue being thrashed out at the Council of Jerusalem would define the very shape of Christianity as grace won out over the prevailing legalism. For, while 'special revelation' had been crucial in the matter of the mission to the Gentiles, no special revelation was necessary to support the centrality of caring for the poor! The poor were clearly already in the apostles' hearts and minds – they were central to their ministry.

In gathering funds for poverty alleviation in Jerusalem, Paul laid down certain guidelines:

- One should give as much as one can (1 Cor 16:2; 2 Cor 8:2);
- Such giving is voluntary (2 Cor 8:3, 8), not legalistic;
- The principle of equality should apply (2 Cor 8:13–15).

The principle of 'equality'

In 2 Corinthians 8:13–15 Paul says the following:

Our desire is not that others might be relieved while you are hard pressed, but that there might be equality. At the present time your plenty will supply what they need, so that in turn their plenty will supply what you need. Then there will be equality, as it is written: 'He who gathered much did not have too much, and he who gathered little did not have too little.'

These verses appear in the context of Paul's urging the Christians in Achaia to join their Macedonian brothers in providing relief aid to the church in Judea. The Greek word for equality here is ισότης *(isótēs)* which designates equality in a quantitative sense, as might be used, for instance, for equal sums of money, shares or pieces. Equality was one of the key characteristics that the Greeks ascribed to true friendship, a valued ideal demanding the sharing of things. Here Paul affirms that such sharing is not intended to impoverish those who are giving; such relief aid is not to leave the givers hard pressed. The equality that Paul speaks of here, in the context of his concern for the poverty of Christians in Jerusalem, essentially involves equal relief from the burden of want.

Paul indicates that this kind of sharing is intended to be mutual so that, while the Christians in Jerusalem were in urgent need of relief aid at this time, Paul envisaged a time when this might be reversed. And indeed, in his letter to the Romans, Paul pointed out that the Gentile Christians in Macedonia and Achaia had already in a different sense received much from those in Judea:

*For Macedonia and Achaia were pleased to make a
contribution for the poor among the saints in Jerusalem.
They were pleased to do it, and indeed they owe it to them.
For if the Gentiles have shared in the Jews' spiritual
blessings, they owe it to the Jews' to share with them
their material blessings.*
(Rom 15:26–27)

Although the language of 'equality' was Greek, Paul supports the principle by referring to the story of God's provision of the manna for his people while they were journeying through the wilderness. He makes this reference by quoting directly from Exodus 16:18 in the Septuagint. In referring to the manna narrative, Paul places the emphasis on equality in terms of seeing that everyone's basic necessities are met.

While God provided the manna, each person had the duty to gather manna to feed those in their tent:

*This is what the LORD has commanded: 'Each one is to
gather as much as he needs. Take an omer for each person
you have in your tent.' The Israelites did as they were told;*

some gathered much, some little. And when they measured it by the omer, he who gathered much did not have too much, and he who gathered little did not have too little. Each one gathered as much as he needed.
(Ex 16:16-18)

While some may have had the ability and industriousness to gather more than they needed, others may not have gathered enough. However, as they measured out what they had gathered so as to provide an omer of manna for each person, those who had a surplus would provide out of this surplus for those who did not have enough.

Moses went on to instruct the Israelites not to hoard their surplus, and indeed there was no point in hoarding, for any surplus that was hoarded would simply decay:

Then Moses said to them, 'No one is to keep any of it until morning.' However, some of them paid no attention to Moses; they kept part of it until morning, but it was full of maggots and began to smell. So Moses was angry with them.
(Ex 16:19–20)

Surely it is Paul's intention, in referring to this account in Exodus, to highlight to his readers that God provides adequately for his people, but that the meeting of everyone's basic needs requires those who have gathered a surplus to share out of their plenty with those who are in need. With reference to this same passage, Randy Alcorn[24] highlights how easy it is to embrace a wrong individualistic understanding of the resources that God has entrusted to our care:

[24]Randy Alcorn, *Money, Possessions and Eternity,* p239

Imagine Christ multiplying the five loaves and two fish, and the disciples accumulating the proceeds until they were buried underneath, while the masses went unfed. It's a bizarre scenario, yet how easily we bury ourselves in the resources God has handed to us, while the needs of the world go unmet. We assume that God has multiplied our assets so we can keep them, when in fact he has multiplied them so we can distribute them.

In essence what Paul does is to take Jesus' teaching on care for the poor and ensure that it would not only have application in taking care of local needs known first hand. Paul clearly extends the application of Jesus' teaching to the trans-local level where relief aid can be provided between churches that are geographically remote from one another.

What is more, Paul's personal involvement in facilitating the provision of relief aid gave this a strongly relational aspect, for Paul was known to both the Christians in Jerusalem and to those who were providing the aid in Macedonia, Achaia and elsewhere. He was personally supervising a process that could be fraught with difficulties – for the church in Jerusalem was not immune to controversy surrounding issues of poverty relief as evidenced in the opening verses of Acts 6.

Certainly, there was much at stake. What was at issue was not merely the need to ensure that there was equality with regard to the provision of basic necessities. Paul had an abiding concern for the one new man in Christ whom he writes about so passionately in his letter to the Ephesians, and it is attitudes of paternalism, entitlement or donor-dependency that can do great damage if aid is not extended with much wisdom and genuine depth of relationship. Paul was determined that there should be no sense of superiority and inferiority in the relationship between Jewish and Gentile believers, writing full of conviction to the Galatians:

'There is neither Jew nor Greek, slave nor free, male nor female, for you are all one in Christ Jesus' (Gal 3:28).

The New Testament Church embraced all – rich and poor, slave and free, Jew and Gentile. The only criterion for inclusion in God's mission was God's redeeming and transforming work of grace in the person's life. Paul lived this out to the full, as he embraced people like Onesimus, the runaway slave, to serve alongside him, no longer as a slave but as a genuine brother in Christ.

A radical ethos of caring for the poor and needy both within and outside the Church

In demonstrating the love and justice of God, the Scriptures indicate that the Church has, first of all, a basic responsibility towards the poor and needy in its own ranks (Rom 12:13; Jas 2:15–16; 1 Jn 3:17–18). Widows and orphans get a special mention in the New Testament letters (Jas 1:27; 1 Tim 5:3–10). However, in Galatians 6:10, Christians are urged not merely to do good to fellow believers, but to do good to all people. Such a sentiment is also present in the first few verses of Hebrews 13, where the instruction to 'keep on loving each other as brothers' (Heb 13:1), is expanded by the inclusion of a call not to forget to entertain strangers, and to remember and identify with those in prison and with those who are ill-treated.

The New Testament Church clearly lived out such teaching and demonstrated a truly radical ethos of caring for the poor and needy, both within and beyond the Church. This ethos continued to characterise the Church for centuries.

The testimony of Church history

Right down through the centuries of Church history, the Church has often taken a leading role in caring for the needy in the wider community beyond its membership. Thus, for example, there is evidence that by AD 250 the church at Rome supported some 1500 needy persons in a way that was otherwise unheard of in the late Roman Empire.[25] In the following century the Roman emperor Julian tellingly complained about Christians (whom he called Galileans) as follows: 'The impious Galileans support not only their own poor but ours as well; everyone can see that our people lack aid from us.'[26]

Until the development of the welfare state in the West and state socialism in some other parts of the world during the past century, the Church was often the only institution that provided care for the poor and places of refuge for the sick and dying, for the ill-treated and for travellers. During times when there were outbreaks of the plague, Christians were known for coming into the cities to help the dying, rather than fleeing from the cities to save their own lives. Helping the poor set Christians apart, showing the world that they cared and operated according to a radically different value system.

Paul's instructions to Timothy were to teach Christians to cultivate generosity on the one hand, and simplicity with contentment on the other (1 Tim 6:6–10, 17–19). In the early centuries of the Church, leaders like Augustine, Cyprian, Origen and Chrysostom took this to heart and taught that one should spend on oneself only that which was absolutely necessary, and the remainder should be given for the care of the poor. Consequently, a radical ethos of sharing pervaded the early Church and continued to make its mark down

[25]Ronald Sider, *Rich Christians in an Age of Hunger*, p88
[26]Randy Alcorn, *Money, Possessions and Eternity*, p226

THE NEW TESTAMENT CHURCH'S RESPONSE TO POVERTY

through the centuries. Many centuries later, John Wesley held the view that any Christian who takes for himself anything more than the plain necessities of life lives in an open, habitual denial of the Lord. Indeed, Wesley gave most of his income away, wearing inexpensive clothes and eating only simple food. He wrote: 'If I leave behind me ten pounds, you and all mankind bear witness against me that I lived and died a thief and a robber.'[27]

Holistic mission: no false dichotomy

In his ministry, Jesus addressed the needs of the whole person, both spiritual and physical. In the Church down through the centuries this holistic approach to ministry, which embraced both evangelism and social concern, has been faithfully emulated – until the twentieth century that is. For centuries social programmes were viewed as a natural outgrowth of the regenerative work of Christ and salvation, and churches pursued serving the poor as an integral outworking of Christian discipleship. In the nineteenth century, evangelical Christians were at the very forefront of social reform and, in England, for example, evangelicals like William Wilberforce (1759–1833) and Lord Shaftesbury (1801–1885) championed respectively the causes of abolishing the slave trade and reforming working conditions in factories and mines (especially for women and children).

However, in the twentieth century an unbiblical polarisation between evangelism and social concern took place. This was unfortunate, for the failure to embrace a holistic approach to evangelism and social concern as integrally part of God's intentions for his Church produced an imbalance. The reality is that, 'if we only promote and practice one "wing" of the gospel, it is like an eagle

---

[27]Ronald Sider, *Rich Christians in an Age of Hunger*, p190

attempting to fly with only one wing.'[28]

How did this polarisation between evangelism and social concern develop? In the period 1900–1930 much of the social concern by evangelical Christians was eliminated in what has sometimes been termed the *Great Reversal*. This happened mainly as a reaction to the rise of a 'social gospel'. In evangelical Christian circles an increasing stigma was attached to being associated in any way with a 'social gospel' and, by inference, with theological liberalism.

The term 'social gospel' originally referred to formulations of the gospel made by Christians in North America in situations of great poverty and deprivation in the latter part of the nineteenth century. This social gospel stressed the compassion of Jesus, and emphasised the Christian obligation to respond to people's physical needs and oppression, and follow Jesus' example by doing good works. There was an optimism that the progress being made would see the world become a better and better place, and that humanity would through its own efforts bring in God's kingdom of justice and peace. The social gospel tended to overlook personal sin and the need for repentance and salvation, while emphasising the role of doing good works.

The reaction to the social gospel was to go to the other extreme, with evangelicals and conservatives emphasising spiritual needs, evangelism and the future heavenly aspects of the kingdom of God. With the social gospel, the divinity of Christ had come under attack. In attempting to affirm that divinity, opponents of the social gospel lost the balance between the human and divine natures of Jesus. Many evangelicals therefore began to use the term 'social gospel' as a means of labelling as unorthodox any views which highlighted the social dimension of the gospel. The result was that such defenders of the faith began to separate

[28]CRUDAN, *Christian Wholistic Development*, p40

evangelism and social concern, word and deed, spirit and body.

This dichotomy took root within the core beliefs of Christians and affected how they viewed all of life. For those that emphasised the spiritual dimension, their primary interest was the salvation of people's souls. Salvation was viewed primarily in individualistic and personal terms. More emphasis was laid on personal sins than on social sins (like structural injustice and oppressive systems). Sin was viewed mainly vertically in terms of offence against God, while the horizontal dimension of offence against one's neighbour or God's creation tended to be neglected. On the other hand, those who emphasised the physical dimension focused on transforming the social structures of society so that the world would be a better place in which to live. Sin was perceived primarily as social injustice; personal sin tended to be neglected. The goal was to see society restructured socially, politically and economically, but the role which personal salvation played was minimised.

While this polarisation has been characteristic of Christian perspectives for much of the twentieth century, things have gradually been changing over the past few decades. Among evangelicals there has been a recovery of the understanding that the gospel of Jesus Christ has inescapable social implications. In this regard the Lausanne Covenant[29] represented a significant milestone. At Lausanne, in 1974, the 'International Congress on World Evangelisation' focused on the nature and urgency of the evangelistic task. John Stott spoke of mission as the Church's sacrificial service to the world, which includes both evangelism and social action, and this broader understanding was enshrined in the Covenant. At the same

[29]The Lausanne Covenant arose from the 'International Congress on World Evangelisation' which gathered some 2700 evangelicals from 150 countries in Lausanne, Switzerland in July 1974 under the leadership of Billy Graham

time speakers from the Two Thirds World – in particular René Padilla and Samuel Escobar – had a tremendous impact on the Congress. Padilla and Escobar were anxious lest the Congress would instigate a programme of evangelisation using Western marketing techniques which, for the sake of numerical success, would ignore the social implications of repentance. The Covenant reflected this concern, warning against concealing the cost of discipleship and affirming that socio-political involvement was part of a Christian's duty. It acknowledged that churches have sometimes been in bondage to culture rather than seeking to be faithful to the Scriptures, and it declared that Christians should share God's concern for reconciliation throughout human society and for liberation from oppression.[30]

In July 1989, Lausanne II was held in Manila in the Philippines. The Manila Manifesto which was produced, like the Lausanne Covenant, affirmed the primacy of evangelism but added that 'Jesus not only proclaimed the kingdom of God, he also demonstrated its arrival by works of mercy and power'. Hence, it asserted, 'we are called today to a similar integration of words and deeds.'[31]

Significant progress has been made in evangelical circles towards eliminating the polarisation between evangelism and social action, as both Christ's divinity and his humanity are more fully grasped. Both his divinity and his humanity are foundational for *orthodoxy* (right beliefs) and *orthopraxis* (right conduct). It is in Christ's humanity, his identification with human beings, his hunger, his pain and his compassion that the Church gets its motivation for humanitarian action and service to others. If this is overlooked, as evangelicals had tended to do during much of the twentieth century, then meeting the physical needs of others becomes devalued.

[30] *New Dictionary of Christian Ethics and Pastoral Theology,* p538
[31] *Ibid,* p538

The consequences of this are spelt out as follows in *Christian Wholistic Development*,[32] a document produced by the Christian Rural and Urban Development Association of Nigeria (CRUDAN):

The mentality of 'preach the gospel, win the lost and then all social ills will gradually vanish as the number of believers in society increases' distorts the gospel and as we have seen here in Africa, does not match the realities that we see. Some call this the 'trickle down effect', others have called it the 'redemption and lift' theology. It suggests that the answer to poverty lies in people just becoming Christians. We do not want to underestimate the effect of true conversions on society, but alone it cannot respond effectively to the degree of poverty that we face.

In addition to that, poverty is not just caused by individuals living irresponsibly; structural and institutional sin or evil are also a reality. Therefore not just individual effort is needed but responses on a more macro level (seeking to impact a much larger number of people) are necessary to address the structural issues. The gulf between poverty and a satisfactory standard of living for all is just too wide for individuals alone to bridge. Moreover, Christ teaches about both righteousness and justice, commitment to both the King and the Kingdom.

This document goes on to lament the fact that, because of a false dichotomy between the spiritual and the material, social action has unfortunately been viewed as both a lesser priority and as something that people can essentially do by themselves, whereas evangelism is seen as something 'spiritual'. The truth is, however, that social action is just as dependent on God's grace as evangelism:

[32]CRUDAN, *Christian Wholistic Development*, p6–7

Ultimately, transforming people and communities and society at large is something only God can do. Our role is to discern what God is doing and obediently join in. Because of this significant fact, we learn that God is not asking us to be successful, only obedient. We are not authors of change, nor even the primary actors. It is the action of God that will ultimately bring about true, lasting change. Our role is vitally important but we need to have the humility to recognise that through our own efforts, we are quite unable to bring about God's purposes. If there is to be any human transformation that is sustainable, it will be because of the action of the Holy Spirit, not the effectiveness of our development technology or the cleverness of our participatory processes.[33]

Social ministry must be seen as an essential partner to evangelism if we are to embrace a truly biblical understanding of God's mission. It is all part of one seamless garment. In reality evangelism and social activity 'are like the two blades of a pair of scissors or the two wings of a bird, as they were in the public ministry of Jesus. The partnership is, in reality, a marriage.'[34]

An appropriate response today

What do we learn from the New Testament Church's response to the poor? First and foremost, the way in which the New Testament Church embraced the poor is a great inspiration. The poor and needy were seen as indispensable to the Church community; without their inclusion and participation the stamp of authenticity was missing. The remarkable solidarity between rich and poor, slave and free, Jew and Gentile, which was rooted in the knowledge that entrance into God's Kingdom is the same for all – an

[33]CRUDAN, *Christian Wholistic Development*, p50
[34]John Stott, *Issues Facing Christians Today*, p340

acknowledgement of one's spiritual poverty and one's need of the Saviour – inspires us to stand together. For, without Christ we are all poor. But in Christ we all equally have access to the riches of God's grace and his blessings, and are caught up in God's purposes, in his glorious mission.

From the New Testament example, it is clear that the Church itself is to be the locus for caring for the poor. They did not franchise this out, nor did they drift into a false dichotomy between evangelism and social concern. The Church's response to the poor was holistic. The gospel was preached and the needy were cared for – both within the Church, as a matter of priority, and beyond. The biblical standard is that evangelism and social concern are integrally linked. They belong together like the two wings of a bird, as evidenced in the public ministry of Jesus, who both preached the good news of the Kingdom and cared for the needy, healing the sick and feeding the hungry.

In pursuing this, *relationship* is key – loving, caring relationships, in obedience to Jesus Christ by the power of the Holy Spirit. This is what distinguishes Christian involvement in poverty alleviation from secular initiatives. It is not simply a matter of throwing resources at a particular context of poverty. Rather, it is a genuine heart-felt invitation from those who have received God's mercy: 'Come with us and we will do you good' (Num 10:29). It's all about drawing others who are poor and in need into God's community of faith, so that they in turn will be caught up in God's great mission.

Chapter 3

The importance of keeping the gospel central in embracing the poor

Steven Oliver

In the presence of God and of Christ Jesus, who will judge the living and the dead, and in view of his appearing and his kingdom, I give you this charge: Preach the Word; be prepared in season and out of season.
(2 Tim 4:1-2)

Introduction

We have been powerfully provoked and biblically convinced that we, as a family of churches, are mandated to 'remember the poor' (Gal 2:10) if we are to fulfil our God-given task of discipling all the nations of the earth.

Over many decades there has been an ongoing debate as to whether this means that acts of compassion are to be the major thrust in serving the poor, or whether this is to include evangelism as the main focus. Some have gone so far as to say that aiming to lead people to Christ through mercy ministry displays a wrong motivation, with such acts of compassion being used merely as 'bait'.

In this chapter, I will argue that the gospel is the most important service that we can ever bring to the poor.

It is important to note that C. Peter Wagner[35], in his book *Churchquake*, writes:

> *I continue to argue that prioritising the cultural mandate [ministry to the poor – no evangelistic thrust at all] over the evangelistic mandate [serving the poor with the intention of leading them to Christ] was, in all probability, the major cause of the decline of mainline denominations during the past thirty years, beginning in 1965. If the evangelistic mandate is kept a priority, social service [ministry to the poor] can be maximised. However, if the cultural mandate is given equal or greater priority, both will suffer.*

Clearly his studies of various church denominations and movements have shown the effects of keeping **the gospel central to our mission to the poor.**

In keeping the gospel central to our ministry with the poor, we are faced with some challenges which must be carefully considered in our quest to be truly New Testament in nature. Some of these are:

- making sure that all our apostolic teams are biblically convinced that we are to serve the poor;
- ensuring that there are sound apostolic foundations in all of our social action projects which will see that the gospel remains central to our ministry to the poor;
- establishing clear mandates and vision statements for each project within the Church that clearly prioritise the gospel before other ministry activities;
- fully integrating our evangelism initiatives and works among the poor;
- not compromising our evangelism thrust in order to

[35]C. Peter Wagner, *Churchquake*, p195

raise funds from secular institutions;
- maintaining a 'sharpness' in every project with regard to the presentation of the gospel;
- training each and every project member to be able to deliver a clear gospel message;
- concentrating on keeping each ministry closely knitted into the Church body so that 'independence' does not creep in;
- not allowing the registration of a project as an NGO (Non Governmental Organisation) or PBO (Public Benefit Organisation) to distance it from direct oversight by the elders.

These are but a few challenges we must overcome in our eagerness to keep the gospel central to our work among the poor. In an interview, Steve Chalke stated: 'I think the old evangelism and social care "dualism" needs to go. Until recently, we had an evangelism department and a social care department. These need to be fully integrated.'

The fact that 'the word became flesh' (Jn 1:14) and dwelt among us most certainly shatters any illusion that the spiritual and the physical can be separated. In his ministry, Jesus did not simply concentrate on meeting the needs associated with just one dimension of life while neglecting others. Rather, he met the needs of the whole person. By contrast, as David Adams has pointed out in the second chapter of this book, an unbiblical polarisation between evangelism and social concern took place during the twentieth century. This was very unfortunate, for the failure to embrace a holistic approach to evangelism and social concern as integrally part of God's intentions for his Church produced an imbalance. The truth is that, 'if we only promote and practice one "wing" of the gospel, it is like an eagle attempting to fly with one wing.'[36]

---

[36]CRUDAN, *Christian Wholistic Development*, p40

In light of these thoughts, we will now consider the gospel and its impact in ministering to the poor.

The eternal consequences of the gospel

Let us turn our attention to the necessity of keeping the gospel central to our work among the poor as we consider the eternal consequences of the gospel.

What good is it for a man to gain the whole world, and yet
lose or forfeit his very self?
(Lk 9:25)

First, we need to take note of the high value of the soul. Nothing in the entire world comes near to the value of one soul. Likewise, Jesus insisted that it is better to destroy the physical body than to fall into sin and separation from God (Matt 5:29). Also, in the parable of the lost sheep, he expresses his heart for the individual, which once again highlights the true value of an individual soul through Jesus' eyes (Matt 18:13). One gets a very clear sense that Jesus adopted primarily an eschatological view when it came to the needs of the flesh and the soul.

Second, true fulfilment for a person can be found only in Jesus, which highlights the fact that the world and all its pleasures can never have the same lasting effect. Therefore, acts of mercy are limited in their benefit to the recipient. We read that the disciples marvelled at the fact that demons fled as a result of their ministry, but Jesus highlights an act of greater importance when he urges them rather to 'rejoice that your names are written in heaven' (Lk 10:20). Here Jesus directs them to what should be the true goal of our activity in the community.

In Matthew 6:20, Jesus also highlights the fact that our

efforts on earth should concentrate on activities 'where moth and rust do not destroy'. Added to this, we need to consider the reality of heaven and hell. Charles Spurgeon pointed out that the more of heaven we have in our lives, the less of earth we will covet. The goodness of our salvation brings:

- reconciliation with God;
- the fullness of the Holy Spirit;
- life in God;
- the promise of heaven;
- adoption into his family;
- the cleansing of guilt and shame;
- sanctification;
- joy, liberty and freedom;
- eternal fellowship with God… and many more blessings.

Whereas, the reality of eternal damnation brings:

- eternal suffering;
- helplessness;
- eternal separation from God.

Charles Spurgeon's view of hell is worth considering, when he urged his hearers to remember that there is a place where the spirits are forever paying their debt to divine justice. Considering the facts detailed above, how can we ever think of meeting only the physical needs of the poor without sharing the good news which has been entrusted to us?

Compelled to preach!

It is our clear understanding that Jesus ushered in the Kingdom of God when he became flesh among us. When instructing his disciples to continue the task he had started, he commanded them to 'go and make disciples of all nations' (Matt 28:19). This is the primary task given to us – to make his salvation plans known to all mankind. In taking this message to the nations, we serve the poor.

There is a very clear focus to the task entrusted to us. Paul clearly understood this when he stated: 'Yet when I preach the gospel, I cannot boast, for I am compelled to preach. Woe to me if I do not preach the gospel!' (1 Cor 9:16). As we reach out to those in need around us, we are similarly compelled to preach the gospel of salvation.

Our responsibility for the opportunities afforded us

Not only was Paul compelled by the love of God to preach the gospel at every opportunity, but one gains further insight into his motivation in 2 Corinthians 5:10–11:

> *For we must all appear before the judgment seat*
> *of Christ, that each one may receive what is due to him*
> *for the things done while in the body, whether good or bad.*
> *Since, then, we know what it is to fear the Lord,*
> *we try to persuade men.*

This understanding would surely be part of the reason for Paul saying, 'Woe to me if I do not preach the gospel!' Paul seems to understand that he would have to give an account to Christ for every opportunity he had had to preach the good news. This he seems to have taken very seriously.

Furthermore, Paul's instruction to Timothy indicates a clear mandate to be ready to present the gospel in every given opportunity when he writes: 'In the presence of God and of Christ Jesus, who will judge the living and the dead, and in view of his appearing and his kingdom, I give you this charge: Preach the Word; be prepared in season and out of season' (2 Tim 4:1–2).

If we accept our responsibility as Paul did, we would never contemplate a social action initiative without taking advantage of preaching the gospel.

Effects on rewards

Even though we are encouraged to do so, we so often feel uncomfortable about seeking God's rewards for our actions here on earth. Rewards clearly seem to be a further motivation for Paul as he took the gospel to the ends of the earth (see Matt 6:19–21; Col 3:23–24). Paul wanted the prize! 'Run in such a way as to get the prize' (1 Cor 9:24). Paul worked hard at preaching the gospel as it had a direct result on the prize he would ultimately receive.

Opportunity beckons!

Approximately two-thirds of the world's population live in the 10/40 Window (that section of the earth's surface that stretches across Africa and Asia between latitudes 10 and 40 degrees north of the equator). Some 85% of those living in the 10/40 Window are among the poorest of the world's poor, while some 90% of the people living in the 10/40 Window are unreached and unevangelised.[37] Therefore, we have one of the greatest opportunities to preach the gospel among the poor.[38]

Simon Pettit charged us in 1998, saying, 'if we are to see the masses swept into the church, then we must remember the poor.' Let us not miss our opportunity.

Simon Pettit's message compelling us to 'remember the poor' had a deep and lasting impact on my life and ministry. For some time I had held the opinion that God had called us to serve the poor through the alleviation of poverty. However, I have come to realise that this is only half the story. During a prayer time with some friends, in which we were seeking God on behalf of the poor, God spoke to us very clearly:

[37]Howard Culbertson, on the Southern Nazarene University website: http://home.snu.edu/~HCULBERT/1040.htm
[38]In a message entitled, 'Remember the Poor', delivered at the *Newfrontiers* Leaders' Conference in Brighton, England, 1998.

I have called you to serve the poor, by not only releasing them from the evil effects of poverty, but also empowering them to participate as co-equal members of the body of Christ, its ministry and mission to the nations.

While I had been passionate about working hard to see the poor released from poverty and all of its evil effects, and I had been diligent in building them into the life of our local church, I now began to realise what a wonderful gift and a remarkable resource God was providing to enable us to fulfil our calling and desire to reach many nations. By nature the poor are a mobile people and this is an exceptional benefit in reaching the nations. As I have learnt, they also have an amazing ability to adapt to other cultures and practices.

As we embrace our mandate to the poor, receive them into our churches, empower them and equip them, then we will be able to release them into the nations. My greatest joy has been to release to other churches some of those who have come from humble beginnings, but who have responded to the opportunities afforded them and have become co-equal participants in our mission.

Paul clearly understood the power of the finished work of Christ in totally transforming an individual when he appealed to Philemon to receive back Onesimus, the runaway slave, 'not as a slave but as a dear brother' (Philem 16). Paul had no doubt that, through the right discipleship and given the right opportunities, the poor can achieve mighty things in God. With current globalisation, more and more of the world's population are on the move. We can therefore expect many more foreigners to show up at our churches and many will be poor. If we respond to them as Paul responded to the runaway slave Onesimus, we are likely to plant and resource many more churches around the world. What extremely good news it is for the poor that they can participate in our mission to the nations that God has called us to!

Practical considerations

If we accept this mandate, then there are some practical considerations that will impact our way of doing things. Let us consider a few:

- **The right foundation**

Before initiating a new ministry to the poor, we need to ensure that the first priority of this action is to reach the lost. I would suggest that it should stand out in the mission statement and become an absolute for that initiative.

- **Prioritised evangelism training**

Each participant of the new social action team must receive both theological and practical training on how to present the gospel. It would also be an advantage if they were exposed to an evangelist who in turn would impart a heart for reaching the lost. Their attendance at evangelism training conferences (like, for example, the *Newfrontiers* initiative, Front Edge) would also be an added benefit.

- **Faith prayers**

A constant reliance on prayer builds ongoing expectation that team members will see those they are serving being saved. It is important that leaders involve themselves in this task and also give joyous thanks for those added to the kingdom of God.

- **Leadership involvement and ownership**

This aspect has a great influence on the effectiveness and success of any social action project. Leaders need continuously to maintain a high expectation that the teams will see souls saved. Ongoing and regular

meetings where success can be measured are a vital tool in keeping the gospel at the forefront of the social action.
- **Recording and measuring results**

It would further be advised to set 'faith goals' which lift expectation, and then to employ a suitable method of recording results. Once again, rejoicing over positive results is a must!
- **Apostolic stamp of approval**

The apostolic call to churches and individuals to serve the poor must be suitably worded and communicated so that evangelism is adequately highlighted. It must always give the impression that we are engaged in this wonderful task to see individuals added to the kingdom of God.

Conclusion

Many of the roots of poverty are as a result of sin. If this is the case, then the gospel is the answer to releasing people from poverty.

Chapter 4
Apostolic ministry and the poor

Martyn Dunsford

Introduction

The purpose of this chapter is to consider biblically the role and responsibilities of the apostolic team toward the poor, especially in the context of gospel extension and establishing churches in the nations.

Apostolic background

Old Covenant roots

The original apostles would have been well acquainted with the extensive Old Testament scripture passages which present God's attitude to the poor and the responsibilities on God's people to care for the poor. This is well covered by David Adams in the first chapter of this book, but we will just note here some of the significant points.

1.   God is presented as a God of compassion and justice (Ex 34:6; Ps 145:8–9; 89:14; 97:2) who has a special place in his heart and will actively intervene on behalf of the poor, afflicted and oppressed (1 Sam 2:8; Jer 20:13). Many Old Testament prophetic words about the coming Messiah and his Kingdom reign specifically emphasise these characteristics (Is 9:6–7; 11:1–5).

2.   There are many warnings about God's anger towards those who oppress or even just fail to help the poor and victims of injustice (Is 10:1–4; Jer 5:26–29).

3.   Special mention is made of widows and orphans (fatherless), and often the 'alien' (those from a different ethnic or cultural background, not a member of God's people) is specifically highlighted (Ex 22:21–23; Deut 15:18–19). God's people are instructed to give generously to the poor (Deut 15:10–11; Ps 112:9). A special mention is also made of justice, food, clothing and shelter (Is 58:6–7).

4.   God instituted laws to protect poor people from the worst ravages of poverty (Ex 23:10–11; Lev 19:9–10; Deut 23:19–20) indicating that the people of God had a collective responsibility for such welfare.

With Jesus

Not only would the early apostles have had such a traditional background awareness and sense of responsibility for the poor, but these same things would have been dynamically conveyed and reinforced by the words and works of Jesus himself with regard to the poor.

1.   As prophesied in the Old Testament, Jesus perfectly demonstrated what the compassion and justice of God would mean, in practice, for the poor. He was able to say that the Spirit of the Lord had anointed him to preach good news to the poor, to proclaim freedom for the captives, sight for the blind and release for the oppressed (Lk 4:18–19). And then in response to John the Baptist's enquiry he could say what he had actually done as a result of this anointing:

*Go back and report to John what you hear and see: the blind
receive sight, the lame walk, those with leprosy are cured,
the deaf hear, the dead are raised, and the good news
is preached to the poor.*
(Matt 11:4–5)

Jesus saw the people he ministered to as 'harassed and helpless, like sheep without a shepherd' (Matt 9:36). This presents us with a picture of the crowds of people on whom Jesus had such compassion, as people unable to cope, overcome with life's pressures, if not victims of injustice then certainly of their circumstances, powerless to help themselves. Not only did he preach the good news of the Kingdom to them, inspiring hope for the future through faith in God, but he also healed every disease and sickness. In such a graphic context Jesus' words to them would have dramatically impacted their lives forever:

*The harvest is plentiful but the workers are few.
Ask the Lord of the harvest, therefore, to send out workers
into his harvest field.*
(Matt 9:37–38)

Healing was one of the main ways in which Jesus ministered to the poor because it not only alleviated suffering but also mitigated injustice, at the very least the injustice of indifference, disdain and using people for one's own advantage. When Jesus healed the man with the shrivelled arm, the Pharisees had no care about the man; just how they might use the situation against Jesus (Matt 12:9–13). Little wonder Jesus was angry and deeply distressed at their stubborn hearts (Mk 3:5). After this Jesus withdrew but the crowds still followed him and he healed them all, remarkably fulfilling Isaiah's prophecy (Matt 12:15–21; Is 42:1–4).

Jesus, God's servant in whom he delights, through the anointing of the Spirit, will proclaim justice to the nations, not by dispute, but with gentleness and faithfulness, not breaking the bruised reed or snuffing out the smouldering wick (what a picture of the care and tenderness of this beautiful servant). He will establish justice on the earth and through this, and in his name, the nations will put their hope. Following on in the Isaiah passage God the creator and giver of life says to his people that he has called us in righteousness and takes hold of our hand for us to be representatives of his covenant with the people and a light to the Gentiles (nations), to open blind eyes, free the captives and release those who sit in darkness and in dungeons (Is 42:5-7). The early apostles may not have realised it at the time (eventually it got through) that the ministry that Jesus started was to be taken to the nations by them. And furthermore, just as Jesus never limited the prophetic words about his ministry only to the spiritual needs of humanity, but ministered to their physical, material and circumstantial situations as well, neither could the early apostles, nor we today, restrict our Kingdom extension activities to the spiritual. Indeed as we seek to reach the nations we should be especially concerned to bring the healing and justice of God to all the people in all the places, wherever God leads us to serve him.

Can the feeding of the five thousand, a miracle which followed teaching about the Kingdom of God and healing everyone who needed healing, and which was a practical provision of food for the hungry (Lk 9:10–17), be understood as a challenge to us similarly to provide practically for the needy?

If we are unable to heal the sick or work miracles, or only manage to do it on a small scale at the moment (God help us to increase in these things!), we certainly can still demonstrate the kingdom of God through our gentleness and tender care of the broken, weak and disempowered, and to the best of our ability provide practical help for them too.

2.   As in the Old Testament Jesus also warned the selfish rich about the coming judgement (Lk 6:24–25). The parables of the rich man and Lazarus (Lk 16:19–31) and the sheep and the goats (Matt 25:1–46) graphically emphasise this.

3.   All needy people were ministered to by Jesus. Serving the Lord is presented as intensely practical care activities for the needy; the hungry, thirsty, those needing shelter or clothing, those in prison or sick and the stranger (surely a connection with the 'alien' in the Old Testament) are all specifically mentioned. The parable of the Good Samaritan extends this care to those of different ethnic and religious backgrounds (Lk 10:25–37), and even to the 'extreme' of giving to one's enemies (Lk 6:27–36). Jesus had a special place in his heart for children (Matt 19:13–15) and a special concern for his soon-to-be-bereaved, widowed mother (Jn 19:25–27). He gave regularly to the poor from the common purse that he and his disciples kept (Jn 13:29).

4.   Lastly, it is clear that Jesus gave much teaching about giving and stewardship generally, usually in the context of caring for the poor. It is interesting to note that whereas instructions on giving in the Old Testament focused on the amount (tithing), Jesus focused on the attitudes with

which we should give, including the following:

- Giving to the poor should be discrete and private, not broadcast around to receive the praise of man (note this is described as an act of righteousness. 'Almsgiving' in KJV, and 'righteousness' could equally be translated and understood in terms of 'justice').
- We need to be free from the power of money and materialism (Matt 6:24), placing more value on treasure in heaven than earthly possessions, and so give to the poor (Lk 12:32–34), not allowing worldly wealth to prevent obedience to God as in the case of the rich man (Matt 19:16–30).
- We need to have a free and generous attitude with respect to our possessions so we can give or loan to others, not even necessarily expecting to be repaid (Matt 5:42; Lk 6:30–35).
- Giving is not to be legalistic religious duty while neglecting mercy and faithfulness (Matt 23:23).
- Giving to the poor is not to become more important than giving worship to Jesus (Matt 26:6–13).
- Giving sacrificially. The poor widow gave all she had (Mk 12:41–44).
- Giving with a sowing and reaping mentality, i.e. with faith to receive more back in order to keep giving (Lk 6:38).
- Wise stewardship of resources is required for which God holds us accountable (Lk 19:11–27).
- Trustworthiness is to be proved in handling worldly wealth or possessions, however little, before being entrusted with the true spiritual riches of the kingdom (Lk 16:10–12).

Apostolic injunction – 'Remember the poor'

With this background in mind it is not at all surprising that care for the poor features so prominently in the early Church. It seems that the Jerusalem church was birthed in conditions of poverty with many of its members extremely poor. There was a remarkable application of Jesus' teachings in the church there, to the point that it was noted that 'there were no needy persons among them' (Acts 4:34). To those tempted to speculate that numbers of poor folk were attracted to the church purely because of the material help they would receive, it is worth noting that the early chapters of Acts focus not on the possible advantages taken of the church, but on the enthusiastic and infectious generosity of both the members and the apostolic leadership of the church. Naturally and without question the needs of the poor were attended to. They did not view care of the poor as a project that they might or might not initiate or engage with. It was not simply an outreach strategy that could possibly contribute towards church growth. They accepted they had a responsibility to care for the poor with the same compassion and sense of justice that God has. It was never in their thinking that preaching the gospel, building the church, etc. was a separate issue and certainly not in conflict with meeting the needs of the poor.

These things are all mentioned as working out alongside each other in the early Church. Teaching, fellowship, prayer, the miraculous, giving to the needy, meeting together, praising God and church growth are all described, in that order, as activities of the Jerusalem church (Acts 2:42–46). Later on similar things were mentioned: sharing with each other, testifying to the resurrection with great power, much grace on them all, no needy persons among them, gifts laid at the apostles' feet and distributed to those in need (Acts 4:32–35).

Other points worth noting in the early Church:

1. There was an incredible degree of unity and together-ness among the believers with the associated attitude of common ownership of possessions leading to liberal giving and sharing with one another (Acts 2:44; 4:32).

2. It would seem that capital reserves or excess assets were donated or sold in order to give to the poor. The disciples still retained their own homes in which they met (Acts 2:46) and Mark's mother still had her own home (Acts 12:12). A communal lifestyle is not indicated here, but a sense of community with a sense of mutual responsibility for one another.

3. There were no rules or obligations imposed on people to give or sell up. There was no problem with Ananias and Sapphira owning property; their problem was in deceiving the apostles about how much they sold it for (Acts 5:1–10).

4. It seems that believers both shared with the poor at their own discretion (Acts 4:32) and also brought special donations that they 'put at the apostles' feet', which were then distributed to the needy (Acts 4:35,37; 6:2). Giving to the poor was therefore a joyful, perhaps spontaneous, activity by the believers. But meeting the needs of the poor was also a carefully organised activity for which the church leadership took responsibility.

5. Special prominence is given to the daily distribution of food to the widows indicating the extreme nature of the needs regularly and continuously provided for

(Acts 6:1–7). This was a church leadership responsibility which required substantial organisation. But there were complaints that the Grecian Jewish widows were being overlooked in favour of the Hebrew Jewish widows. This was almost certainly not a deliberate discrimination, because the apostles then took pains to carefully address the issue. This was not an abdication of responsibility but a careful delegation of responsibility to men full of the Spirit and wisdom, so that the needs of the poor widows might continue to be met, but in a fair and unbiased way. The apostles were not neglectful towards these widows, nor did they view it as being less important than the ministry of the word and prayer. Both the needs of the poor widows and the ministry of the word and prayer continued in such an effective way that the word of God spread and the number of disciples increased.

Clearly to the apostles, who walked and talked with Jesus, care for the poor was a central feature of their ministry, which was reflected in the Jerusalem church that they led in its early years.

When Paul came on the scene they were careful to work through with him the important issues pertaining to the recognition of his apostolic ministry such as a) the content of his gospel, b) that God was evidently at work in his ministry, c) his calling to the Gentiles and d) the grace of God given to him to be an apostle. In this context they particularly wanted also to ensure that he (and Barnabas) would 'remember the poor', which Paul was obviously already doing and was eager to continue to do (Gal 2:1–10). Surely this apostolic injunction was given to emphasise the fact that a significant aspect of apostolic ministry is to care for the poor.

They might also have been impressing on Paul that the Gentiles he would reach through his apostolic ministry should remember that they had a responsibility back to the Jewish poor. Indeed Paul embraced such a principle by arranging offerings from Gentile churches for the Jewish poor of Jerusalem and he specifically referred to such an obligation as a reason for arranging such offerings:

> *For if the Gentiles have shared in the Jews'*
> *spiritual blessings, they owe it to the Jews to share*
> *with them their material blessings*
> *(Rom 15:27).*

More on this later but at the very least it indicates an apostolic responsibility to care for the poor cross-culturally and trans-nationally, as well as for the poor in their own localities.

Apostolic example

In his personal life and ministry Paul demonstrated a commitment to helping the weak as a response to Jesus' exhortation that it is more blessed to give than to receive. He was able to do this simply through the hard work of his own hands to earn money to support himself, his co-workers and then giving away the rest (Acts 20:34–35). He then taught others to follow this example (2 Thess 3:7) by living productive, hardworking lives to provide for their own daily necessities, not to be dependant on others, and so to be in a position to share with those in need (Eph 4:28; 1 Thess 4:11; Titus 3:14).

Paul himself was a tentmaker by profession and he worked as such when necessary (Acts 18:3). In Corinth he worked hard with his own hands (1 Cor 4:12) and in

Thessalonica he put up with toil and hardship, working day and night so he would not be a burden to them (1 Thess 2:9; 2 Thess 3:8).

It was important to Paul that, in contexts where the Church was already stretched trying to meet the needs of the poor, he should not be an additional burden on their resources. So he made every effort to ensure that funds were not diverted from the poor to himself, but rather in fact that the reverse would happen.

At the same time he was clear that he had a right to such support (2 Thess 3:9), just as others, whose ministry demands that they give themselves fully to the work of the gospel, can expect the church to provide adequately for them (1 Cor 9:14; 1 Tim 5:17). In fact, when Paul was in Thessalonica the Philippian church sent him support several times when he was in need, even in his troubles as he described them (Phil 4:14–19). As we have seen above, he didn't just sit back and expect gifts to come to him; instead he also worked hard with his hands to make ends meet, and here we can begin to understand his apostolic example.

When Paul said, 'I can do everything through him who gives me strength' (Phil 4:13), it was in this context. At times he had plenty, at times he was in need, at times well fed, at times hungry, at times adequately supplied, at times in want, but content in any and every situation. The important thing to him though was still to do everything that God had called him to do; this was his focus and goal. And he was not going to be deflected from doing it by lack of resources nor be distracted from doing it in times of plenty when he might be tempted to relax. This determination to fulfil all that God had called him to do, whatever it took, was the essence of his apostolic faith. Whatever the means of provision, whether through his own hard work or by receiving church support, he carried on his ministry, and through it all he was

careful not to neglect sharing what he had with the poor –
what an example and challenge for apostolic teams today.

Just as an aside, Paul gave other reasons as well for
declining the right to expect church support, including the
following:

1. To receive the personal reward or blessing of being
   able to offer the gospel free of charge (1 Cor 9:15–18).

2. To demonstrate that God's grace is sufficient to provide
   for him in whatever situation of need or weakness (2
   Cor 12:9–10).

3. To set an example of being hardworking as a rebuke to
   the idle. There were obviously some in the
   Thessalonian church who expected to be looked after
   and fed, but who were well able to provide for
   themselves. Hence the instruction that, if they will not
   work, they shall not eat (2 Thess 3:6–10). However, the
   truly weak should receive assistance (1 Thess 5:14).

4. To expose false ministers of the gospel. There will be
   deceiving and false ministers who are covetous and
   try to exploit the Church (2 Cor 11:1–20; 2 Pet
   2:1–3,13–16). Hence there is a special requirement for
   true ministers of the gospel to be free from the love
   and pursuit of money (1 Tim 3:3,8; 6:11).

Apostolic foundations of a local church

When apostles / apostolic teams are laying the foundations
of a local church (1 Cor 3:10) they should seek to include the
dimension of care for the poor as a significant foundational
feature of church life. This involves the following:

1. Apostolic teaching should establish believers firmly

in the grace of God and in the way they live it out in practice, both individually and corporately. Teaching also shapes the overall life of the church in terms of its practices and priorities. Ministry with the poor should be taught in such a way that believers will understand and embrace God's heart for the poor and that compassion, faith and generosity of spirit towards the poor characterise the normal life of the church. Believers should engage in actions and activities, both spontaneously and planned, that will be a blessing to the poor, and this becomes a rich seam of God's grace that runs through the heart of the church.

2. Apostolic appointment and ongoing influence on the leaders of the church so that they take on board their responsibility to encourage and manage ministry with the poor through the local church. The church should seek to provide for the basic necessities of life for its poor members, examples being the widows' situation highlighted in Acts 6 and 1 Timothy 5. This responsibility will sometimes necessitate initiating specific ongoing sustainable programmes to meet the needs of the poor.

Local church leaders should also be open to apostolic requests to take up offerings for the poor in other places (Rom 15:25–27; 1 Cor 16:1–4) which demonstrates that we belong to one another and care for one another as 'a chosen people, a royal priesthood, a holy nation, a people belonging to God' (1 Peter 2:9). We are part of the worldwide body of Christ, the global family of God, and as such we have a responsibility for one another. Who better than the itinerant apostolic teams, who travel around the churches and connect them together through close and affectionate relationships, to bring to the attention of and make requests of church leaders for the poor in other places and nations? I will write more about this below.

3. There is also a prophetic dimension to the foundations of a local church (Eph 2:20). Prophetic ministry is part of the overall ministry of the apostolic team and it brings with revelatory impact an understanding of the purposes and ways of God. It inspires faith which produces commitment to a course of action; it imparts the courage and conviction necessary to do a work for God; it creates a sense of intentionality, and there is excitement and expectancy in the air. Prophetic ministry brings direction, and decision-making becomes clear, which is not based on human wisdom or natural evaluation of the situation, etc. (although it is important to research thoroughly and understand all the implications of what you are about to do), but rather on what God is telling you to do.

Ministry with the poor needs this prophetic input because it stirs up people to action in accordance with the specific guidance of God for that church. This is what happened in Antioch when the prophet Agabus predicted a famine and the church then sent a gift to help their brothers living in Judea (Acts 11:27–30). When faced with so much need in the world today, how we need this prophetic direction as to exactly what we should engage with! Incidentally it is interesting to note that Agabus himself did not insist on the Antioch believers helping out financially. He brought the revelation and no doubt stirred up a spirit of compassion, but the decision to do it was taken by the church itself. Prophetic ministry does not override the authority of the local elders to make decisions and govern generally the local church, but it does bring the word of God to which a response must be made.

4. When considering exactly what the apostles would have taught in terms of church responsibilities for the poor, the following summary of the previous section might be helpful:
   - The local church should recognise that it has a basic minimum responsibility to seek to provide for the daily necessities of life for its 'poor'members.
   - The poor in the church family should be prioritised (Rom 12:13; Jas 2:15–16) but beyond that, as we have opportunity, we should do good to all people (Gal 6:10; Heb 13:2,16).
   - Beyond the local church it is important to respond to the needs of the saints, and then all other people, in other regions or nations as God directs and enables.
   - The poor would be generally recognised as those who are unable to help themselves, specifically noting that widows, orphans, the sick, those in prison, victims of injustice and strangers (those from other ethnic, cultural or religious backgrounds, even our 'enemies') could most obviously come into this definition.
   - The level of provision should be at least the basic necessities of life, i.e. food, drink, clothing, shelter, personal visiting, friendship and hospitality and maybe directly financial when necessary.
   - There necessarily needs to be an evaluation of the need before giving. The following factors will figure in considerations:
     ▸ Can the proposed recipient meet his own needs?

The idle should not be rewarded with charity but the truly weak should receive assistance (2 Thess 3:10; 1 Thess 5:14).

▶ Is the proposed recipient's lifestyle characterised by godliness and service in the church, like the widows in 1 Timothy 5:3–10?

▶ Is there a devotion to the fellowship and unity of the church? (Acts 2:42–47)

▶ Are there other believing family members who could meet their need? (1 Tim 5:4)

▶ When considering the boundaries of what could be regarded as daily necessities, is it wise stewardship of the church's resources? (Lk 16:10–12; 1 Cor 4:2)

▶ Is it fair or does it discriminate against some? (Acts 6:1–6)

• Godly attitudes are so important. We should treat the needy with understanding and consideration imagining ourselves in the same predicament (Heb 13:3), and be merciful rather than judgmental when considering those in need (Jas 2:12–13). The uncaring rich are warned (Jas 5:1–6) and, instead of being arrogant etc., told they should be generous and share with the poor, thereby laying up treasures for themselves in the coming age (1 Tim 6:17–19).

It is a serious offence to show favouritism towards the rich and discriminate against the poor (Jas 2:1–3) and it was utterly hypocritical of the Corinthian church to declare outwardly their unity by breaking bread together, while in reality there were divisions between the rich and the poor, who had nothing and went hungry (1 Cor 11:17–22).

5. It is worth mentioning that apostles don't have to be experts on setting up and managing social care projects for the poor today with all the required legal, financial and technical skills qualifications. Their task as we have seen is to bring the 'pattern' or the 'form' of sound teaching (2 Tim 1:13; Rom 6:17) reinforced by the example they set which provides a pattern of conduct to follow (Phil 3:17). Paul's way of life agreed with what he taught (1 Cor 4:17). Apostles established the principles of teachings or traditions of practically caring for the poor (2 Thess 2:15; 3:6).

The exact situations they were faced with in the early Church, especially it would seem in the example of on-going provision for widows (Acts 6:1–6; 1 Tim 3:2–16), may not be relevant in our modern-day contexts. We have to address the needs we face in culturally appropriate ways but according to biblical principles, which modern-day apostles with their wisdom and understanding of the ways of God should help to apply.

For example, it is interesting to note the way in which slavery was addressed in the early Church. The Old Testament background in Jewish society regarding slavery usually viewed it as an economic issue and, compared to nations around, was extremely compassionate. A Hebrew debt slave should be freed after six years and he should then even be given gifts to help him survive thereafter. It could well have been the case that he was treated so well in slavery that he might well be inclined to remain in that situation (Deut 15:12–18).

Slaves who converted to Christianity would have found great hope and encouragement in the way Jesus had identified with the poor and marginalised, becoming a servant himself. The apostles in the early Church, apart from condemning slave traders (1 Tim 1:10), did not challenge the evils of slavery in terms of explicitly advocating its abolition. They certainly did, however, address the issue in terms of how Christians, both slave owners and slaves themselves, should live. The distinction between slave and free in the Christian community should be removed (Gal 3:28; Col 3:11). However slaves should obey their masters (Col 3:22), and respect them (1 Tim 6:1). And slave owners should provide what is fair and right for their slaves (Col 4:1). Paul wrote to Philemon about his runaway slave Onesimus, who had become a Christian, to receive him back not as a slave but a dear brother (Philem 15–16).

These instructions may well not apply within the Christian community today, where the focus of Christian activity has become more to do with the abolition of slavery in the world and rescue of those still entrapped in it. Apostles won't necessarily be at the forefront of such campaigns and projects (unless specifically called to do so), but they will be involved in advising churches and individuals as to how they might or might not be engaged in it. They will do this, as already noted, according to biblical principles, and with guidance to people according to their faith and consciences, where scripture is silent or unclear as to exactly what to do in practice. This is a little like guidance on issues such as eating habits or recognising some days as special, etc. (Rom 14:1–18).

6. In conclusion to this section it is worth commenting further on the issue that it is not the task of apostles / apostolic teams to dictate exactly what the local church

should do with respect to the poor. Ultimately it is up to the elders of the local church to take responsibility and make decisions, and to implement actions which will be of assistance to the poor. The picture that emerges from the early Church in the New Testament is one of affectionate, stimulating relationships between the apostolic and local church elders, which result in unity of heart and mind in reaching agreements together about what should be done.

Having set a powerful example and having taught thoroughly with respect to the poor, with prophetic encouragement, Paul's other main method to influence local church elders would be to appeal to them on the basis of his personal relationship with them (2 Cor 10:1), not commanding them but giving them advice (2 Cor 8:8,10). A great example of this is when he wrote to Philemon, his dear friend and fellow worker, for whom he gave thanks and whose love had given him great joy and encouragement. With this kind of affectionate language he then came to the point about how he wanted Philemon to treat his runaway slave Onesimus, who had now become a believer through contact with Paul.

Although in Christ I could be bold and order you to do what you should do, yet I appeal to you on the basis of love. I then, as Paul – an old man and now also a prisoner of Christ Jesus – I appeal to you for my son Onesimus, who became my son while I was in chains...
I am sending him – who is my very heart – back to you… no longer as a slave, but better than a slave, as a dear brother… Welcome him as you would welcome me.
(Philem 8–10, 12, 16–17)

How could Paul have been resisted after those words?

Apostolic family of churches

Considerable prominence is given in the New Testament to the special offerings taken up by the Galatian, Achaian and Macedonian churches for the poor in Jerusalem. It seemed to be of special significance for Paul who assumed personal responsibility in all the arrangements for this important example of trans-national and cross-cultural care for the poor. He clearly regarded this not as an option for local churches but as an obligation, and he took pains to ensure it took place not only with godly and generous attitudes, but also giving attention to the practical arrangements of taking up the offerings and transporting them to Jerusalem, ensuring harmony and transparency. This surely indicates a priority of apostolic ministry (see Acts 24:17; Rom 15:23–29; 1 Cor 16:1–4; 2 Cor 8 & 9).

The New Testament churches were clearly well connected to each other, with strong relational links. There was a family atmosphere between the churches, a sense of belonging to one another as the people of God. Practically the links grew out of the relationship they had with the apostles and their teams who were involved in establishing them in the first place and subsequently travelled around them. Indeed Paul's apostolic team drew in people from these various churches who travelled and ministered with him for various lengths of time (as, for example, in Acts 20:4). Paul's letters are full of affection with warm greetings and information being sent, requests for prayer, and personal details mentioned, clearly demonstrating the friendly family atmosphere that existed between them (e.g. Rom 14:1–16; Phil 4:21–22; Col 4:7–8; 2 Tim 4:19–22).

In this context it would have been a natural part of apostolic ministry, completely in keeping with the focus of their ministry among the churches, to assume responsibility to ensure that churches were aware of the poor in other churches in other places and cultures, and that they fulfilled their obligation to care for them trans-locally. Apostles should be active in this matter, and the principles Paul drew attention to in the specific offerings mentioned above should still apply to the church today. These principles can be set out as follows:

1. The space given to this in the New Testament, the care taken to place this practice in a substantial theological framework, the attention given to the practical details and the evident desire of significant brothers to be associated with this trans-national and cross-cultural care for the poor, all indicate that this is a 'big deal' issue to be taken seriously by apostles today.

2. This was not just about giving money to the poor. Indeed the word for money is not even used in these passages. It's all to do with the grace of God outworked in the life of these local churches. The grace of God was given to them in such measure (2 Cor 9:14) that they overflowed with joy in severe trials and rich generosity in extreme poverty (2 Cor 8:1, 2). These wonderfully blessed churches saw that it was a privilege to share in the service of care for the poor (v.4). It is described as an act of grace (v.6) and the grace of giving (v.7). Their model in giving was the grace of the Lord Jesus Christ (v.9) and their relationship with the apostolic team provided a channel for this grace to become operative (v.4–5).

3. Paul was also concerned with the issue of equality between the churches. We do not understand this to mean that living standards were to be the same everywhere, but that all received at least the basic

necessities of life in their own context. Even though the Galatian, Achaian and Macedonian churches were very poor themselves, Paul was able to recognise that the saints in Jerusalem were in even greater need, so that assistance should flow in that direction. Maybe at another time it would flow the other way (2 Cor 8:13–15). Who better than apostles, with their wider experience and knowledge of situations, to make godly assessments in this issue of equality, and to be credible when appealing for help on this basis?

4. Another principle that Paul adhered to was that those who have sowed spiritual seed should receive the benefit of a material harvest – indeed it was even a right (1 Cor 9:11,12). So the Gentile churches of his day who had shared in the Jews' spiritual blessings, owed it to the Jews to share with them their material blessings (Rom 15:26,27). Paul had a particular sensitivity regarding this Gentile-to-Jew obligation, even asking for prayer that this service for them might be acceptable to them (Rom 15:31). Whatever the particular issues and sensitivities then, we are on safe ground now to adopt the principle that those churches blessed materially should be specially concerned to care for the poor in contexts that have blessed them spiritually.

5. It is also part of the apostolic remit to ensure that the handling of such offerings for the poor will be above criticism (2 Cor 8:20,21). Paul was at pains not to pressurise people emotionally in that he did not command them to give, but rather advised them (2 Cor 8:8,10). Also he encouraged them to give thoughtfully and carefully over a period of time (1 Cor

16:1–4; 2 Cor 9:7), not just as a spontaneous response. Plurality in decision-making and the actual handling of cash would also ensure transparency (1 Cor 16:4; 2 Cor 8:16–24).

6. Lastly apostles will want to see all this done to the glory of God. They want to honour the Lord in this way (2 Cor 8:19) and ensure that the focus of thanksgiving and praise for such giving is directed towards God (2 Cor 9:11–13). They want to stir up faith through consideration of the grace of our Lord Jesus Christ and what God will release for us now in terms of Kingdom resources.

For you know the grace of our Lord Jesus Christ, that
though he was rich, yet for your sakes he became poor,
so that you through his poverty might become rich.
(2 Cor 8:9)

And God is able to make all grace abound to you, so that
in all things at all times, having all that you need, you
will abound in every good work.
(2 Cor 9:8)

You will be made rich in every way so that you can be
generous on every occasion, and through us your
generosity will result in thanksgiving to God.
(2 Cor 9:11)

Thanks be to God for his indescribable gift!
(2 Cor 9:15)

Trans-national and cross-cultural giving to the poor is a great thing to do in the eyes of God and for his glory. It's one aspect among many others, but an important aspect nevertheless of the grace of God being outworked in the life of the local church, prompted and encouraged by apostolic ministry.

Apostolic extension – reaching the nations

Apostolic ministry in the New Testament was at the forefront of extending the Kingdom increasingly around the world. They fulfilled the Great Commission by preaching the gospel, gathering believers together and making disciples in the context of planting new churches and establishing them on firm foundations.

As we have seen already, ministry to the poor was an integral part of this great work, necessarily so because of the large numbers of poor people in every place. The poor responded readily to the gospel of hope, that God loved and cared for them, that he was their helper, healer and provider in time of need. So the churches inevitably had significant proportions of poor people as members. This is reflected in the many references and injunctions in the letters, most of which we have already considered, as to how the poor should be treated (and also how the rich should behave).

However there is no suggestion in Acts that a particular apostolic strategy to reach into a new area was to identify and focus on bringing the gospel primarily to a particular group of poor people. In fact Paul seems to prioritise reaching major regional cities, rather than the poorer rural areas. Paul also made it a particular priority for himself, in the early days of the Church when the centre of gravity was shifting from Jew to Gentile, to preach first in the synagogue to the Jews (e.g. Acts 14:2; 17:2; etc.) without focusing particularly on the poor. Care for the poor was particularly outworked within the local church for its own members and then beyond, rather than as a strategy when on apostolic mission. In fact, there are many people of substance, both in public and economic positions, mentioned as being among the first reached by the gospel – for example, Sergius Paulus, proconsul in Cyprus (Acts 14:7), Lydia, businesswoman in Philippi but from Thyatira (Acts 16:14), not a few prominent women in Thessalonica (Acts 17:4), Dionysius, a member of the Areopagus in Athens, and Damaris (Acts 17:34), Erastus, the city of Corinth's director of public works, and Gaius from Corinth whose hospitality the whole church there enjoyed (Rom 16:24,25).

Gaius must have been well-off to have offered such hospitality, as must have been all the other people mentioned in whose homes various churches met, such as Priscilla and Aquila in Rome (Rom 16:3) and Ephesus (1 Cor 16:19), Nympha in Laodicea (Col 4:15), and Philemon (Philem 2), among others.

Perhaps these kinds of people could be regarded in the category of 'worthy persons' (Matt 10:11) or 'men of peace' (Lk 10:6) whom Jesus referred to in his instructions to his disciples as he sent them out on preaching trips when he was with them (Matt 10:5–17; Lk 9:1–6; 10:1–12). If we seek to apply these instructions to apostolic teams reaching new nations, then the emphasis is clearly on preaching, healing and searching out such worthy people to provide operational bases, which would then naturally become the base for ongoing church work and fellowship. They were to take no financial or material provision for their ongoing needs, but trust God for his supply, which again would reinforce the idea that they were not to focus on the material needs of the poor. Rather, as in Jesus' ministry, the harassed, the helpless, the oppressed, the sick and the poor were to be reached primarily through the ministry of the Word and the Spirit.

However, when considering those who might be regarded as 'worthy people', there are two remarkable incidents recorded in Acts which connect them directly with care for the poor, apostolic ministry and significant gospel breakthrough – Simon in Joppa (Acts 9:43) and Cornelius in Caesarea (Acts 10:1).

In the first case, believing for a miracle, Peter had been sent for to pray for a lady called Dorcas who had just died. The significant thing here was that Dorcas was well-known for doing good and caring for the poor. The widows gathered together to show Peter the clothes she had made for them, to demonstrate that her compassion for the poor marked her as a special person warranting the attention of Peter, and God, was pleased to raise her from the dead. Subsequently many people in Joppa turned to the Lord and Peter stayed there with Simon the tanner for some time (Acts 9:32–43). No doubt this became the focus of a growing church in Joppa.

In the second instance, the God-fearing Gentile, Cornelius, was also noted by God because he prayed regularly and gave generously to the poor. An angel came to him in a vision, telling him his prayers and gifts to the poor had come up as a memorial offering before God. He was told by the angel to send for Peter while he was staying with Simon the tanner in Joppa. At the same time Peter was having a life-changing encounter with God preparing him to go and preach to the Gentiles, which was completely contrary to his Jewish traditions. As a result the gospel came for the first time to the Gentiles, and the Holy Spirit was also poured out on them (Acts 10).

What can we glean from these two instances, where surely it is not too strong to say that care for the poor is mentioned as the main factor which initiates the supernatural activity of God resulting in remarkable salvation breakthroughs? Indeed, in the latter case, through the most resistant cross-cultural barrier of the day, from Jew to Gentile. True compassion for the poor is so in tune with the heart of God, it is not surprising to see such sovereign and supernatural works of God in contexts where it is taking place. Is it too much to extract from these stories the truth that ministry to the poor is such a powerful demonstration of the grace of God that it can open doors for apostolic mission to take place – salvation, church planting and reaching new nations?

In the first instance, where believers are already serving the poor in some context, apostolic ministry comes in on the back of that to greatly extend the Kingdom, as in Joppa. In the second case, apostolic ministry in regions beyond seeks out or is led to a Cornelius-like 'worthy person', even though an unbeliever, who is prepared to receive the gospel because he has already had his heart opened by the compassion of God for the poor. Apostles should be alert to and recognise the grace of God at work in preparing people and opening doors for the gospel in this way, even if it is not a planned strategy of theirs for Kingdom extension.

Apostolic reproduction from among the poor

The anointing that was on Jesus, and that we ought also to seek, was not just to preach good news to the poor but to proclaim freedom for the prisoners and to release the oppressed (Lk 4:18–19). The poor are not just a category of people that need always to be on the receiving end of help and assistance. Instead the aim should be to see them set free from the ravages of sin, sickness, poverty, oppression and, released from the chains that bind them into a life of little or no opportunity, to rise up and be self-sufficient and then to go and help others. They should be lifted up to live productive and fruitful lives in the service of the King. Surely this would be the most wonderful demonstration of the grace of God in a poor person's life – redeemed from slavery to sin, released from the curse of poverty and oppression, and raised up as a servant of the most high, called into ministry that will redeem and release many others.

Is not this what 'the incomparable riches of his grace' is all about, being saved from sin, not *by* good works but *for* good works? We should recognise that the poorest of the poor are also being worked on by God, created in Christ Jesus to do the good works that God prepared in advance from them to do (Eph 2:6–10).

Surely it is the poor more than any other who, when delivered from a life of always being at the receiving end, can demonstrate most effectively the truth and power of Jesus' words quoted by Paul, 'it is more blessed to give than to receive' (Acts 20:35)!

Is this not how the poor become rich – through 'the grace of our Lord Jesus Christ, that though he was rich, yet for your sakes he became poor, so that you through his poverty might become rich' (2 Cor 8:9)? Has not God chosen those who are poor in the eyes of the world to be rich in faith and to inherit the Kingdom he promised to those who love him (Jas 2:5)? We can expect and look for the redeemed poor to be among those who, with great faith, fearlessness and self-sacrifice, will be at the forefront of those who not only inherit the Kingdom but preach it and demonstrate it among the nations.

Not many are called from those who are wise by human standards, influential or of noble birth. But God chooses the foolish to shame the wise, the weak to shame the strong, the lowly and despised, those things that are not, to nullify the things that are (1 Cor 1:26–28). How much in keeping with the ways of God will it be to see an army of foolish 'have nots' and 'are nots' raised up to demonstrate his glory in the earth!

Like David of old, whom God took from the obscurity and lowliness of being a shepherd boy, to become a great king whose kingdom and throne prefigured that of his Greater Son to come (2 Sam 7:8–16), so we can expect God to 'stoop down to make great' (Ps 18:35) the lowly and poor of our generation, and raise them up to do greater things in the kingdom. He delights to raise the poor from the dust and lift the needy from the ash heap, to seat them with princes and to inherit a throne of honour (1 Sam 2:8).

He lifts the needy out of their affliction and increases their families like flocks (Ps 107:41). Can we take this as a prophetic indication for us in our apostolic mission that God will redeem and raise up some from among the poor and needy into great apostolic ministries of their own, giving birth to their own families of churches in the poor, as yet unreached, peoples of the world?

Maybe mature apostles should make it a point to search out those from among the poor who have this call of God on their lives, to father and disciple them and to help them in every way into their own ministries.

It is interesting to note that Paul's dearest son in the Lord, Timothy, came from a mixed-race background (Acts 16:1). One could speculate that it possibly disadvantaged him in some respects and maybe this was the cause of his timidity. Certainly in matters of faith his father had little or no positive influence on him, this coming from his grandmother Lois and mother Eunice (2 Tim 1:5). Paul saw the grace of God on his life and became his spiritual father. I wonder how many fatherless kids in the world today, with the right kind of fathering in the faith, will grow into mighty apostles in their own right?

Another 'son' of Paul's, Onesimus, was from a slave background. Paul urged his owner Philemon to welcome Onesimus back in the same way that Philemon regarded Paul as a dear brother and also as a partner (Philem 10–17). This is the same word that was applied to Titus, Paul's co-worker (2 Cor 9:7).

The poor are to be highly regarded not only as dear brothers, but also equal partners and co-workers in the life and ministry of the church, and, for those called, to be empowered to extend the kingdom of God in the nations.

Concluding remarks

Jesus told his famous parable about the Good Samaritan (Lk 10:25–37), not primarily as an exhortation to care for the weak, but in response to the original question, 'What must I do to inherit eternal life?' The questioner answered his own question with the right answer – 'to love God and to love your neighbour as yourself' – but then posed the next question, 'And who is my neighbour?' To the Jew his neighbour was basically equated with family and friends, and the questioner was looking for this reply in order to feel justified that he had 'loved' them and so was worthy of eternal life. Jesus blew this whole idea away and this parable remains a powerful challenge to us today.

Jesus characteristically focused attention on lifestyle attitudes and actions consistent with and worthy of the Kingdom. Not even the question is right! It is not a matter of 'Who is my neighbour?' but 'Who was a neighbour to the poor victim?' Do I live my life in a 'neighbourly' way? Do I really love my neighbour?

Do I truly love and will I really practically help and care for those who are helpless, victims of injustice, despised by others, those of a different race and/or religion, even those regarded as enemies? Taking up my time and money, with nothing in it for me, going out of my way, putting myself at risk, not worrying about my reputation among my peers – this is what it means to be a Good Samaritan.

Is my life worthy of the Kingdom? Will I inherit eternal life? Not, of course, without God's help, especially in this matter of care for the poor.

The importance of this issue in the eyes of God impacts and challenges us from the whole of Scripture. It exposes and breaks our hearts. Our churches need to be touched, moved by the compassion of God and anointed by the Holy Spirit, like Jesus, to preach good news to the poor.

Apostles and prophets need to lead the Church into this service more and more in all the ways we have considered above. It will become an increasingly urgent issue the more we reach out to the world's unreached peoples where the vast majority of the world's poorest people live.

God help us, and to him be all the glory!

Chapter 5

The local church and the poor

John Hosier

Introduction

When we reflect on ministry to the poor many pastor/teachers are generalists rather than specialists. Certainly when we consider the poor, and matters of social and economic justice, we know that we have the specialists. Among the leaders of my previous fellowship at Church of Christ the King in Brighton, we recognised that one of our elders was particularly gifted for this work and also had wide experience which qualified him to oversee our outreach to the homeless of this city. We know that one of our members in another *Newfrontiers* church, a parliamentary candidate, is a specialist and indeed has written a book on the subject. I know some wonderful ladies who have done some amazing work among the poor in the townships of Cape Town. But anyone in church leadership should have some clear views of their own on this subject, even if they are not specialists. This is important if we are to see the church ministering in this area within a clear biblical framework.

Simon Pettit, in his message 'Remember the Poor' to the *Newfrontiers* Leaders' Conference in 1998, clearly taught that if we emphasise apostolic ministry, then alongside the laying of foundations, church planting, raising up of leadership and other things that we may feel should be the fruit of such ministry, there needs also to be a commitment to ministering to the poor. We are to remember the poor.

What I write here, therefore, is in no way intended to address the 'how to' of ministering to the poor. That is clearly the job of the specialists and they should teach us that. Rather I want to attempt a biblical reflection on this subject that can help sharpen our convictions on this issue, release the specialists and give the church confidence.

The statistics

There is probably hardly any other area of life or study where we are so likely to be bombarded with statistics than on the issue of poverty. The statistics are overwhelming and endless – so much so that they probably fail to impact us as they should.

There are the **plain statistics**, for example:

- 800,000 pre-teen girls are prostitutes in Thailand.

There are the **comparative statistics**:

- The world as a whole spends 9 billion dollars a year on water and sanitation for the entire global population; yet Europe alone spends 11 billion dollars a year on ice cream.

There are the **percentage statistics**:

- The richest 20% of the world's population control 86% of the money, which is spent on personal consumption; the poorest 20% spend 1.3% of the money used for private consumption.
- The richest 25% of the world own 87% of the world's vehicles; the poorest 25% own less than 1% of the world's vehicles.

There are the **debt statistics**:

- In the past, certainly, the wealthy nations loaned billions of dollars to the poorest nations but then received back from those poorest nations more than that in debt repayments. Obviously that issue has been highlighted in some very prominent and to some degree successful recent campaigns.

There are the **personal stories**:

- John Kpikpi, a pastor I know in Ghana, offering to move a church member from one lodging to another, found that his total possessions were contained in one plastic bag.

All of us could gather hundreds of statistics like these with the greatest ease. These things are constantly reported. Shocking as these statistics are, the issues they raise are so huge that probably for most people there is the shock of the immediate, but it's not really retained. It's too big, too overwhelming. It's beyond our reach to do anything meaningful about it anyway – or at least that's how we can feel. And although we know that these gross inequalities exist in the world, it's easier to get more emotional about professional footballers getting paid £100,000 a week than it is to get stirred up about the debt problems of Third World nations.

John Stott[39] categorises three groups of poor from the 200 or so references to the poor in the Old Testament:

- First, the *indigent poor*, who lack the bare necessities of life – food, clothing, shelter. In 1 Timothy 6:18 the word σχημα is used. This literally means 'covering'. We could extract from this that shelter, as well as food and clothing, is needed for a person to be content. The economic poor need provision and often employment.
- Second, the *oppressed poor*, who are socially or politically oppressed – the powerless victims of human injustice. The Old Testament prophets, especially Amos, were extremely vocal about this kind

---

[39]John Stott, *Issues Facing Christians Today*, p234

of injustice. Such people need their cause championed.
* Third, the *humble poor.* They are those who acknowledge their helplessness and look to God for salvation. Such people are described in Psalm 34:6.

Why are people poor?

Obviously there is no single or simple answer to this. But the following seem to be among the chief reasons:
* laziness (Prov 10:4; 20:13);
* sin (Prov 23:21);
* family breakdown – the economic implications of divorce and separation;
* war (e.g. the ongoing conflicts in a number of African nations);
* lack of opportunity – millions have no access to education or skills training;
* disasters (e.g. the catastrophic earthquake in Haiti in January 2010);
* a 'catch 22' situation – where one can't get a job without a settled address, but can't get a settled address without money, and there's no job to earn the money!

The results of poverty

Some poverty is caused by personal sin, but poverty also causes sin. Some of the results of poverty are:
* theft (Prov 30:8-9);
* drunkenness – caused by the despair and hopelessness of poverty;
* immorality, such as prostitution;
* disease and early death – diseases like malaria which ravage the poor, who lack access to medical treatment, cause many deaths every year.

When does a person stop being poor?

In a comprehensive way I'd suggest the following:
- when they have sufficient food, clothing and shelter – and the employment to sustain these things;
- when they can obtain justice and are free from exploitation (Prov 22:22);
- when they have come to salvation in Christ.

Therefore, as the people of God, we could ask the following questions:
- Are our hearts moved by the statistics? (Ps 10:17)
- Do we have a concern for the poor as the poor? (Prov 21:13)
- Do we have a concern for the cohesion and welfare of society as a whole, which is actually threatened by the existence of the poor?

The writer Philip Yancey[40] asks: 'Why would God single out the poor for special attention over any other group? What makes the poor deserving of God's concern?' He says he received help from another writer who lists the following 'advantages' to being poor.

1. The poor know they are in urgent need of redemption.
2. The poor know not only their dependence on God and on powerful people, but also their interdependence with one another.
3. The poor rest their security not on things but on people.
4. The poor have no exaggerated sense of their own importance and no exaggerated need of privacy.
5. The poor expect little from competition and much from co-operation.
6. The poor can distinguish between necessities and luxuries.
7. The poor can wait, because they have acquired a kind of dogged patience born of acknowledged dependence.

[40]Philip Yancey, *The Jesus I Never Knew,* p115

8. The fears of the poor are more realistic and less exaggerated, because they already know that one can survive great suffering and want.

9. When the poor have the gospel preached to them, it sounds like good news and not like a threat or a scolding.

10. The poor can respond to the call of the gospel with a certain abandonment and uncomplicated totality because they have so little to lose and are ready for anything.

The Kingdom of God

Any consideration of the needs of the poor, or ministry to the poor, must consider the theology of the Kingdom of God. I understand the Kingdom of God to be the expressed will of God – his rule, government and authority. I also understand that we can view it at three levels:

1. **The Kingdom of God has already come in the person of Jesus.** He personified the Kingdom of God. Where Jesus was, there the will of God was expressed. The ministry of Jesus is the rule of God.

2. **The Kingdom is coming in the present.** The Church is not the Kingdom of God, but it is certainly the agent of the Kingdom in the present age and should be a potent demonstration of God's government. The Church should promote that government in all the earth.

3. **The Kingdom will come in the future with the return of Christ.** At that time we will enjoy the full, comprehensive and everlasting expression of God's rule. Some might speak of that in terms of a millennium, but it can only come fully in the eternal age of the new heavens and new earth.

Because the Kingdom of God should touch every aspect of life – all of which could be examined with benefit in terms of past, present and future – we also see that the Kingdom raises the challenge of the poor.

We can see that in the ministry of Jesus. In Luke 4:16–19 we have the manifesto of the Kingdom. What does the government of God look like? This passage tells us. This reading that Jesus gave from the Book of Isaiah was more than simply the text for the day. It says in verse 20 that the eyes of everyone in the synagogue were fastened on him, which sounds like the preacher's dream! I'd suggest that on this occasion it was the very nature of the reading that drew such interest. What was he going to say next? What he did say was sensational, 'Today this scripture is fulfilled in your hearing' (verse 21). Indeed it was from that time Jesus began to do the works of the Kingdom. So there is a declaration and implementation of government policy.

Consequently, what we find in the New Testament is that Jesus:

- feeds the hungry (e.g. the 5000);
- releases the oppressed (we might think of the demon-possessed or the woman bound by Satan for 18 years);
- heals the outcast (e.g. the lepers).

So we can say the Kingdom has come and it has come to the poor.

When we look into the future and the coming of the Kingdom, we see that there will be no hunger or thirst, but there will be shelter (Rev 7:16). Revelation 21 speaks of a whole new order where all the sufferings and deprivations of the past are done away with, for God declares in verse 5, 'I am making everything new!'

Looking at the ministry of Jesus and then into the future, it seems incontrovertible that the expression of God's will, purpose and government deals with all issues that relate to the poor. For the poor are hungry, oppressed, outcasts. A serious appreciation of the Kingdom of God will inevitably challenge the church, as the agent of the Kingdom as well as an expression of God's rule, to consider her ministry to the poor.

But the Kingdom, rightly understood, will also stop us from being totally overwhelmed. How can we deal with *all* of this? Well, we can't – but there is the fullness of the Kingdom yet to come with the return of Jesus. The Church is the agent to promote and extend the government of God in all areas, including among the poor, but we'll never bring it to consummation and perfection. Only Jesus will do that when he returns.

If I can put it like this: a theology of the Kingdom certainly does not let us off the hook with regard to the poor, but it doesn't impale us on the hook either.

Old Testament and New Testament

Taking a broad look at both the Old Testament and New Testament, I'd suggest that the Old Testament calls for justice with regard to the poor, while the New Testament emphasis is on compassion.

Old Testament

My position is taken from the Book of Amos.

Amos was a prophet from southern Judah who went and ministered in the Northern Kingdom of Israel about 750 BC. It was a time of prosperity in the Northern Kingdom during which period the nation felt politically secure and spiritually strong. The first two chapters of Amos are a brilliant build-up to a denunciation of the Northern Kingdom. One by one, Amos prophesies the judgement of God on Israel's neighbours. Each time he begins with the refrain, 'For three times, even for four'.

So, in turn, he prophesies doom for Damascus, Gaza, Tyre, Sidon, Edom, Ammon and Moab. You can imagine his listeners cheering in wild delight, which would reach an absolute crescendo in Amos 2:4–5 when the Southern Kingdom of Judah is also denounced. That will teach them – well preached, Amos! Imagine then the stunned silence when the crowd realise that Judah is not the climax of the message, but rather it is the Northern Kingdom of Israel itself (2:6a), and notice the reason for the wrath of God that is immediately given – it is because of their treatment of the poor (Amos 2:6–7). This theme recurs again and again:

- 4:1 Materialism – the cry for more and it doesn't matter who gets hurt.
- 5:11 Exploitation of the poor.
- 5:12 No justice for the poor.
- 8:4–6 Corruption, cheating the poor; foreclosing on loans so as to enslave the poor.

What does God want when the poor are so abused?

Well, he certainly doesn't want worship, but he does want justice (see Amos 5:21–24). That is such a telling scripture. Religious worship will not atone for injustice to the poor – God is not impressed. Now that is a helpful link to the New Testament.

New Testament

To me, James 1:27 contains strong echoes of Amos, 'Religion that God our Father accepts as pure and faultless is this: to look after orphans and widows in their distress...'; although the expression 'look after' has more the feel of compassion rather than justice. It is generally accepted that widows in the time of the New Testament would have been poor.

Looking after orphans is exactly what members from my former church in Brighton have been doing among street children in Mexico. Whether or not these children actually have parents alive is a mere technicality; there are tens of thousands of children in many of the big cities of the world today who live on the streets and are, in reality, orphans. Such children live by their wits: they steal; they sell their bodies; they smell and are often ungrateful for what you do for them; they lie and they're diseased. So in some of the big cities, especially in South America, there have been times when they are shot like rats. What the word of God says is that they should be looked after. Whether or not they respond to the gospel, the emphasis is on looking after them. It is interesting to note historically that the early Church used to pick up abandoned babies in the streets of Roman cities and care for them.

When I've been in India I've always been quite wary about giving money to beggars on the streets. Some years ago I was coming out of a shop in Margao in Goa with some money in my hand and there in front of me was a beautiful Indian girl – I should think about seven years old – with a totally naked baby sister resting on her hip. So I gave her the money in my hand, expecting – as a western middle-class man – that there would be some expression of thanks. Instead, as I got into my taxi, there she was – banging on the window, pleading for more. Desperate poverty reduces people to pleading beggars. The appeal of the New Testament is to look after them, not expect something from them.

And how do we handle Luke 12:33 – 'Sell your possessions and give to the poor'? It comes in a passage that tells us not to worry, but to trust God. We tend easily to add to our possessions. Jesus speaks about selling them and giving the money to the poor. The blessing of doing this is twofold. We demonstrate a genuine trust in God and we show compassion to the poor.

This is a very broad sweep, but I'm suggesting that there is a challenge from the Old Testament to consider the issue of *justice* for the poor and powerless. Third World debt is an obvious cause that needs a champion and, of course, both non-Christians and Christians are concerned about that issue. Arguably, we should actively support that, not be neutral about it.

The abortion issue often challenges us for more directly theological reasons of the meaning and sanctity of life. It is again, arguably, an issue that would fall into the realm of justice for the poor – for children in the womb are powerless, and the need is to champion the oppressed. It is probably not wise to work on both sides of this issue at once. There is a need to provide counselling and help for pregnant women considering an abortion. There is also the need to resist the legislation and the clinics that facilitate it. How far Christians should go in such resistance is itself worthy of debate and not irrelevant in the light of attacks made upon abortion clinics and even personnel in the USA in recent years.

The New Testament faces us with the challenge of *compassion*. We may need to define the 'widows' and 'orphans' of our society, but what pleases God is that such people are looked after. In our society we have those who are homeless, drug addicts, victims of abuse, lonely and frightened old people, who, together with others, are the 'widows' and 'orphans' that need to be shown the compassion of Jesus.

I think, however, we must take note of what Peter Wagner[41] says in his book, *Churchquake*:

'My understanding of the scriptures is that Christian social responsibility is, indeed, mandatory, not optional for

---

[41]C. Peter Wagner, *Churchquake,* p195

churches. If the evangelistic mandate is kept as the first priority, social service can be maximised. However if the cultural mandate [by which he means social service / mercy ministry] is given equal or greater priority both will suffer.'

Wagner[42] goes on to quote some examples of major social action by what he calls the 'new apostolic churches' and concludes:

'It is hard for me to resist noting that few local churches that have paraded their theology of patronising the cultural mandate over the evangelistic mandate have ever helped as many poor people year after year as... many other new apostolic churches.'

Indeed, earlier in the book, as he lists seven reasons for the decline of traditional churches, he mentions misplaced priorities and says that in the 1960s the mainstream churches began to change their priorities. The cultural mandate became supreme and the mainstream churches believed it was more important to improve society than to win the lost for Christ. Wagner is reflecting on the situation in America and claims that, probably as a result of this shift in priorities, the mainstream denominations began to decline in 1965.

I remember, a number of years ago now, R.T. Kendall remarking that we hear reports from the mission fields about educational advances and medical care, but where is the report of conversions?

We know that evangelical Christians have been in the forefront of social care and social reform many times in history. But, whenever social care and social reform have become the number one priority, then the church has lost spiritual life and gone into decline.

Economic justice must be a priority for us – the biblical case is undeniable. If we ever allow it to become the priority then I suggest we will have sown the seed for our decline,

[42]C. Peter Wagner, *Churchquake*, p195

which will in time decrease our involvement with the poor.

Remember the poor

Galatians 2:10 is the verse that has been used to remind us that apostolic Christianity does contain the call to minister to the poor. Please remember, at this stage, that I have already spoken of the Kingdom of God, the Old Testament call to justice and the New Testament call to compassion. But I have to point out that the injunction to 'remember the poor' here in Galatians 2 is arguably a reference to the poor in the Christian community.

You will find that both Stott and Lightfoot, in their commentaries, see only this in the verse – it is not understood as being capable of a wider interpretation. Indeed, if we look at the immediate context, it would seem to underline Stott's and Lightfoot's interpretation. At this point in the development of the early Church, apostolic ministry is going to take the brothers in different directions: James and John are now going to concentrate their efforts on the Jews while Paul and Barnabas are going to give their primary attention to the Gentiles – with this provision, that Paul and Barnabas should remember the poor. What poor? The sense is, the poor among the converted Jewish community – the very thing, says Paul, that he was eager to do. For in going to the Gentiles he was eager not to forget the poor of the churches of Judea. 2 Corinthians 8 and 9 remind us that in the following years Paul was raising money from the churches in Macedonia and Achaia for these poorer churches in Judea.

It is therefore relevant and appropriate to consider what responsibility we have to those within the Church as well as to those outside it. For, if a mark of genuine apostolic ministry is that we remember the poor, then the immediate reference would seem to cause us to consider how we look after the community of the saints. Indeed, still in Galatians – chapter 6:10 – we are exhorted to do good to all people, especially to the household of saints. If we are not looking after our own family we hardly have a mandate for looking after those outside the family.

Of course, accounts of what took place in the church at Jerusalem in the earliest days do provide us with a considerable amount of material about looking after the poor within the local church.

- So, in Acts 2:44–45, one of the key elements of the first Church was generosity.
- By Acts 4:34–35 there are no needy persons in the Church because of the generosity of the richer members.
- In Acts 5 Ananias and Sapphira are dropping dead for lying about the money they were bringing to help with the general distribution to the needy.
- By Acts 6 we have the appointment of seven men full of the Holy Spirit and wisdom to ensure a fair distribution of the food handouts among the widows in the church.

I am not trying to build a case against helping the poor outside the church – that would not be a tenable biblical position. I am just trying to underline the point that in the early Church there was considerable effort given to helping the poor within their own community.

My intention is not to take us through a list of 'how-to's' on this issue but simply to raise it:

- How do we identify the poor within our own church?
- How do we express our concern for them?
- How do we minister to them?

With the apostolic ministry of Paul we see there was a continuing concern for the care of the wider family of churches. That concern included the raising of money for some of those churches. This, therefore, is a particular apostolic emphasis – the raising of money from individual churches to help other churches which are poor and needy.

Many have preached sermons on 2 Corinthians 8 and 9 seeking to motivate the Christian community to give generously. Whether it comes to gift days for building programmes, stirrings to help ailing general funds or appeals for mega-offerings at conferences, there is plenty of material we can use from these chapters.

A few verses that perhaps don't always get much attention, but may be of note for our consideration here, are 2 Corinthians 8:13–15, where Paul pleads that there may be some degree of equality demonstrated within the church. Let me put this into a contemporary context for us. Among any family of churches there are many that are poor. Famine or war, say in Africa, may be causing some of those churches to be among the poorest that we know. If we give to those churches, the idea is not to impoverish us to relieve them (there's not exactly much chance of that anyway!) but that there may be a sense of equality. That presents its challenges! It's the sort of issue that has raised acute difficulties in South Africa at times. Do you pay the black pastors in the townships the same as the white pastors in the suburbs? But, however we tackle it, we cannot surely leave some churches in our family in dire poverty while we live in luxury when the call is for equality. Nor, surely, are we doing that.

Response

Again, I'm approaching this in a general way; the detailed approach is for the specialists.

There are poor people within the local church; there are poor churches within any family of churches. The cry of the poor for provision and justice goes up continually from the millions of destitute and powerless around the world. What is our response?

There must be a financial response

We can choose to do nothing and simply remain rich and add to our riches. This is the path of *materialism*. Materialism is not mere possession of material things, but an unhealthy obsession with them. In Scripture we have warnings against a confidence in riches. We have the story of the rich man who filled his barns and then sat back for years of ease, only to find that he disappears into eternity that very night leaving his full barns behind him.

Or, we have the very direct words of Paul:

Command those who are rich in this present world not to be arrogant nor to put their hope in wealth, which is so uncertain, but to put their hope in God, who richly provides us with everything for our enjoyment. Command them to do good, to be rich in good deeds, and to be generous and willing to share. In this way they will lay up treasure for themselves as a firm foundation for the coming age, so that they may take hold of the life that is truly life
(1 Tim 6:17–19).

That passage causes me to raise the question as to whether we are vigorous enough in really encouraging those people who have the ability to make money to make as much as they can and then invest it in the Kingdom of God.

In Luke 16:9 Jesus says, 'I tell you, use worldly wealth to gain friends for yourselves, so that when it is gone, you will be welcomed into eternal dwellings.' This verse comes on the back of the parable about the 'shrewd manager', as the

NIV calls it. Undoubtedly, in my view, this is a parable that is encouraging the children of the light to be shrewd in the handling of spiritual issues including the handling of money. 'Worldly wealth' is a sanitised translation – it should be 'unrighteous mammon'. So what is Jesus saying? Surely, that we should use as an investment in the Kingdom of God what the world so often uses unrighteously and treats as an idol. If the saints who can make money will make money and invest it in mission and ministry to the poor, then when the money is gone (which at the latest is on the investor's death) such people are going to receive a great welcome into heaven. There'll be crowds to meet them, friends they never knew, but because of their investment of money the gospel and compassion reached those in this life who'll be their friends in the next life.

The second approach is to be an ascetic – giving away all we have – which frankly isn't too much of an attraction. The Bible doesn't call us to asceticism. I can't see that Jesus' instructions to the rich young ruler to sell *all* he had and give the money to the poor can be interpreted like that. With that young man, Jesus was testing out what he really wanted. Plenty still want money more than Jesus, but the answer is not a blanket call to asceticism. In its own way, asceticism can be as selfish as materialism. Ascetics tend to be self-absorbed with their own spirituality and are often introspective rather than outward looking. I realise there are exceptions to that, like, for example, Mother Theresa.

If we reject both materialism and asceticism it seems to me that we are left with the biblical way of generosity, which in turn is linked with simplicity. Simplicity is not to be understood as 'nothing' but as 'enough'. When we consider the needs of the poor, and indeed the needs of world mission, then there is a challenge to generosity – something that can always be increased as we simplify our lifestyle.

This is a sensitive area, for simplicity can easily become pharisaical when we begin to bring our opinion and judgment to bear on how others should simplify *their* lifestyle. (And particularly pharisaical if others should suggest how we might simplify *our* lifestyle!) The reality is that we are all extravagant in different ways. Voluntary simplicity of lifestyle is a way to increase our generosity.

God is not glorified when we keep for ourselves (no matter how thankfully) what we ought to be using to alleviate the misery of unevangelised, uneducated, unmedicated and unfed millions.

There must be a 'Body' response

The Bible clearly gives us a way of handling what could be the crippling and overwhelming needs of the world.

As long as there are unsaved people we could argue that we should spend every moment of every day evangelising. But we don't. As long as we have the poor with us (and Jesus says it is *'always'*) we could argue that we continually give away all we have. But we don't.

Surely the Bible's answer to this is the Church – for the Church is the Body with corporate responsibility to do the works of Jesus. The Body is ceaselessly evangelising and ceaselessly giving away and ministering to the poor. With that piece of our theology firmly in place let me suggest that with regard to the poor we especially note the following:

1. **Some members of the Body have a gift of generosity.** If they can also make a lot of money, if they have a position to provide employment, let us encourage them in that.

2. **All of the Body can be challenged about lifestyle.** Not materialism, not asceticism, but generosity

130

combined with simplicity as they are encouraged to contribute to world mission and the poor.

3. **Some members of the Body have a gift of mercy.** These are likely to be the 'hands on' people in ministry to the poor – especially to those outside the Church. It is often gruelling work – there are always setbacks and disappointments. These members of the Body need encouragement from the rest of the Body; they need to be honoured, shown appreciation, pastored and prayed for. From this group probably most will work with the poor. Some will work on behalf of the poor – seeking justice for the powerless.

4. **Encourage the Body in the ministry of hospitality.** You could make a case from Romans 12 that hospitality is a spiritual gift – in reality, some people do seem to have a gift of hospitality. But in context in Romans 12 it is more likely that *'practise hospitality'* is an exhortation given to the whole church.

   However we might define the 'poor' within our church or outside it, they are obvious candidates for hospitality, but who can easily be overlooked because of pressures they could bring – in which case, 1 Peter 4:9 seems particularly relevant: 'Offer hospitality to one another without grumbling'!

5. **Encourage Body ownership.** I have a personal conviction that each local church should 'own' a nation, taking a particular interest in prayer, visits, paying airfares, hosting leaders of that nation in our homes and church. If every church does this, we would cover all the nations.

   Every church could also 'own' a work among the

poor or powerless. The nature of that will vary according to the gifting and resources of that local church. But it is helpful and responsible to own something tangibly that we can affect by prayer, interest, giving and involvement rather than to have a vague concern for all the poor everywhere.

Conclusion

Jesus said, 'You will always have the poor among you' (Jn 12:8); among us in the Church and among us in our society. So we need to consider our responsibilities.

- The statistics are overwhelming.
- But we do believe in extending the Kingdom of God.
- The Bible would call us both to be concerned for justice to the oppressed and to be compassionate to those in need.
- We need to 'remember the poor' in our churches and among our families of churches.
- Our response certainly needs to be financial, but also corporate. We are the Body of Christ who are to do the works of Jesus.

Chapter 6
Pursuing excellence

Nigel Ring

Summary

In this chapter we will consider various aspects of 'good practice', concluding with 20 Key Indicators. These may be used in two ways. First, they provide a helpful checklist for those planning a new ministry. Second, they represent a plumbline against which an existing ministry can be assessed.

Pursuing excellence is about Good Practice. When God looked at everything he had made he was able to declare 'it is good'. So perhaps 'good practice' could be defined as 'God's Practice'!

It is important to note that Good Practice is not an 'absolute', able to be measured by some fixed standard. It is based on experience and knowledge, and is affected by culture and context. There is no 'right' and 'wrong', yet there are practices which would generally be accepted as 'good' based on successful outcomes, 'success' being measured by the positive and beneficial effects on the lives of those involved.

We shall look here at issues which are more about principle than about detailed practice, especially where practice relates to specific sectors such as health and agriculture, or themes such as street children and HIV.

Nevertheless, examples are drawn from sectors and themes where these illustrate principles.

The chapter is divided into three main sections followed by conclusions:

1. What is Good Practice?
2. How does Good Practice apply to people, process and practice?
   - 2.1 *People*
     - **Attitudes**
     - **The gospel**
     - **Participation**
     - **Pastoral care for the teams**
   - 2.2. *Process*
     - **Cross-cutting activities**
     - **The Church**
   - 2.3 *Practice*
3. Key Indicators of Good Practice
   - 3.1 *What are Good Practice Indicators?*
   - 3.2 *How can these Key Indicators be used?*
   - 3.3 *Categories*
     - **Group A – Church and leadership issues**
     - **Group B – Ministry-related matters**
4. Conclusion

Introduction

As Michael walked to work along the dusty and pot-holed streets of Mumbai in India he noticed a group of men and women lying on the pavement under blankets of sacking. Clearly they had slept there all night and even now were waking to a new day of begging in order to stay alive. Like the Levite in the parable of the Good Samaritan he was about to 'pass by on the other side', not wishing to associate with these outcasts who were afflicted with leprosy. But he was alert to God who prompted him to cross over and speak to. them. He quickly learnt that they were about to go down to the sea (which many in Mumbai use as the public toilet) to wash themselves as they were not welcome at the public water points. Michael's heart filled with compassion and thus began Karuna ('Compassion' in Hindi), a ministry of acceptance and care to those affected by leprosy.

Now, ten years later, a mobile clinic parks daily in pre-determined places on the streets of Mumbai. It brings with it clean water for a private shower, a well-equipped medical clinic and a dedicated team ready to serve and share the love of Jesus with those abandoned by society. All who visit would be quick to acknowledge that this ministry carries the qualities of 'good practice'. But what do we mean by 'good practice'?

The purpose of this chapter is to discuss some of the issues related to 'good practice'. Its aim is ultimately to assist churches in being able to carry out 'community development', 'mercy ministries' or 'social action' activities to a high standard. Although these phrases are not synonymous (for instance, social action commonly includes issues of justice and advocacy), they are frequently differentiated more by geography than by definition; 'community development' more common in the southern hemisphere and 'social action' in the northern hemisphere. However, here we shall consider them as interchangeable and use them with reference to helping poor people.

In order to move forward we need to establish some understanding of what the result will look like. This chapter seeks to address the following questions:

1.   What is 'Good Practice'?
2.   How does it apply to people, process and practice?
3.   What practical steps can we take to improve our ministries?

1. What is 'Good Practice'?

Good Practice is God's Practice. As Kingdom people we should seek to do all that we do to a high standard. Was it not God himself who said at the end of every stage of creation, 'It is good'? The gospels teach about good stewardship (e.g. the parable of the talents), which involves people making good use of gifting and resources, and of course caring for people 'wholistically' (I acknowledge this is the less common spelling but this spelling carries the implication of wholeness). God's practice is demonstrated by his love for us. God's love believes for the best and looks to see each person reach the potential for which he or she was created.

How do we earth the phrase 'good practice'? It is a phrase that carries opinion; it is not absolute. So how do we establish ways of improving what we do at present? As we look at what different churches are doing both within the *Newfrontiers* family and outside, and, indeed, what is being done through secular agencies, we recognise there are activities which many would generally acknowledge as being good models (Foundations for Farming formerly Farming God's Way in Zimbabwe, HIV community care in South Africa, Karuna leprosy ministry in India... the list is a long one!). The challenge, however, is to define what the characteristics are that bring us to this conclusion. We shall return to this below. However, suffice to say here that particular models tend to be context-specific. So it is important to understand the biblical principles (e.g. in Foundations for Farming the principles of 'on time', 'no wastage', etc.) rather than to try to 'clone' the model elsewhere. Accordingly, one of the most effective ways of reproducing these models is through training trainers in these principles, rather than the direct teaching of skills to practitioners.

We will begin to unwrap 'good practice' in more detail by considering three distinct categories in which we would expect to find it:

- People – those who are actively involved in transformational development, whether those who are in need or those who are able to bring support and assistance.
- Process and church government – some principles of 'cross-cutting' issues which apply widely in most areas of activity such as planning, monitoring, financial management, training of trainers.
- Practice – those specialist areas in which the core activities of the ministry to people in need are being carried out, e.g. in health, in education, in agriculture.

2. People, process and practice

2.1 *People*
There are two groups of people who are involved in any community development activity; those who are in need, whose situation it is hoped can be transformed in some way, and those who are involved in helping bring about such transformation as 'facilitators'. The health of the relationship between them is critical to the success of any development activity.

Attitudes
The starting point for this relationship must be to address attitude, particularly of the 'facilitator'. For instance, it is easy to adopt a 'giver' / 'receiver' attitude, i.e. 'I have it, you need it, I'll give it'. Although generosity is to be applauded, underlying such a sentiment are power and influence. Where is the participation of the 'recipient' in such an attitude? Does this respect the dignity of the 'recipient'? At

all times we must seek to avoid an attitude which may be interpreted as superior or patronising. Those of us from a colonial background are particularly vulnerable to this!

'Receiver' or 'recipient' must be interpreted through words and phrases such as 'dignity', 'self-esteem', 'self-worth', which recognise the individual or community as people made in the image of God rather than a problem to be solved. Sometimes we refer to people as 'the poor', 'the disabled'. In so doing we are implying that the person is a problem to be solved, thus denying the individual the dignity of being recognised first as a person. Let us be careful to see people as God sees them, made in his image, and treat them as such.

So, 'good practice' with respect to people starts with just that – respect! It must be seen in how relationships are formed and how we interact. There can be a blindness and ignorance to such issues, and training is needed. This was one of the driving motivations for the development of the *Newfrontiers* Life Change Team[43] concept, which has provided an opportunity for individuals to recognise their own weaknesses and vulnerability in their attitudes before finding themselves thrust into a place of ministry where they could, misguidedly, see themselves as the superior party. We must afford the maximum dignity to one another in any relationship and seek to befriend people as Jesus did, seeing the God-image in every man and woman.

Good Practice starts with good relationships,
first with God, then person to person.

The gospel
Next we will consider the underlying distinctive of all that we seek to do. The salvation of both souls and bodies is the

---

[43]Life Change Teams are short-term teams developed by *Newfrontiers* who receive training in cross-cultural ministry from local leaders in-country.

ultimate aim of Christian wholistic development. If we fail to see that the only true transformation is what affects the soul of man, we shall give much energy to improving the outward circumstances without affecting the core issues. Indeed, I am disappointed though not surprised when I hear such well-meaning people as the international economist, Jeffrey Sachs, speaking about poverty relief with unreal optimism about the solution.[44] In common with others he looks for a universal change of attitude which, if it were possible, may well bring about beneficial change. However, as Christians we know that the selfishness of the heart will prevent this happening and it is in the heart where the change must take place.

All social action in a Christian context must include the gospel expressed either in word or deed, or both. Isaiah 61:1–3 gives us the Kingdom mandate that we are to 'bring good news to the poor'. It continues by illustrating the beneficial effects this good news will have; binding up the broken-hearted, setting the captive free, etc. This represents the transforming power of the gospel, the 'secret ingredient' that the Christian has which defines the major difference between what we can bring to a situation compared to a secular aid agency. We may of course need to start with demonstrations of compassion in order to earn the right to be heard.

However, we must guard against only doing acts of mercy. We must also seek opportunity to speak out the truth. The full benefits and fruit of the gospel go beyond 'release' and 'binding up'. There are sustained benefits and goals on offer. Isaiah 61:3 teaches that the previously poor can become 'oaks of righteousness' and verses 4–9 go on to illustrate that the transforming power of the gospel also brings dignity, influence and active participation in the mission of the

[44]2007 BBC Reith lectures

Kingdom. This includes an individual taking ownership of his situation, neither blaming the adverse circumstances on God nor looking to others to solve the problem which, in its extreme, leads to long-term donor dependency. Indeed, 'donor dependency' should be replaced with 'God-dependency' for full and true transformation to be manifest.

> *Good Practice puts the salvation of individuals as the highest goal of transformation.*

Participation

'Local participation is a critical success factor for transformational development' (Myers[45]).

The above relationships open the way to maximum participation in the development process. Participation leads to empowerment. The likelihood of a successful outcome in any development programme is greatly heightened by involvement of potential beneficiaries from the start in charting the way forward and setting the priorities. Such participation fosters that vital ingredient – ownership. In addition, the capacity of individuals is developed and new skills may be learnt. These are all ingredients of sustainability.

However, we do need to recognise there is potential conflict between community participation and Holy Spirit-inspired leadership. While wanting to afford the potential beneficiary of help with the maximum involvement in the transformation process, the techniques such as PLA (Participatory Learning and Action), PEP (Participatory Evaluation Process) or one of the other 'participatory' derivatives may allow a local 'democracy' to make the relevant decisions and negate the activity and leading of the Holy Spirit in directing the best way forward. PLA is

[45]Bryant L. Myers, *Walking with the Poor*, p147

undoubtedly a valuable and effective tool but it must be used with sensitivity to both the physical and spiritual context. Particularly, the facilitator of the process should be alert to the wisdom of the Holy Spirit as he or she empowers the people.

Good Practice involves participation in defining priorities and decision making. Such involvement should lead to capacity building and sustainability.

Pastoral care for the teams

Practitioners who come from outside a situation, or local people who are designated to help carry out a particular activity, need special attention and support. Examples would be those who served people affected by the severe drought in Kenya in 2005/06 or the care of Internally Displaced People (IDPs) in that same nation in 2007/08. They travelled widely and self-sacrificially over many months among those who had been experiencing first starvation, then flooding and finally Rift Valley Fever in 2005/06 and among those severely traumatised by the inter-tribal conflicts of 2007/08. What more demanding and emotionally draining activity can there be than to be 'in the market place' with starving and traumatised people, or among those who are high on drugs or with children who have been abused or abandoned, through the death of their HIV-infected parents? There is often little plaudit for such people as they give of themselves. Good practice demands that we care for and support these teams of practitioners.

Good Practice demands that teams of practitioners receive appropriate emotional, spiritual and physical support.

2.2 Process

Cross-cutting activities

'Process' is used here to refer to cross-cutting activities or skills which are common to many programmes of community development. These should be carried out with a high degree of care and excellence. Some examples are:

- Definition of the need and the anticipated outcomes;
- Resource management including finance;
- Planning and Project Cycle Management;
- Governance;
- Integration with the Church;
- Ministry in the Spirit;
- Team building;
- Training;
- Monitoring, evaluation and accountability.

When Jesus fed the 5000 most of the above were evident (Mk 6:35–44):

- He defined the need – to provide food to 5000 men plus women and children, perhaps 10–20,000 in total.
- He assessed the resources – 5 loaves and 2 fishes.
- He created a plan – to put the people in companies and delegate the distribution through his disciples.
- He managed the activity – establishing his own authority and directing the operation.
- He combined physical need with spiritual activity – 'he looked up to heaven' and exercised faith.
- He built his team – through delegation they were welded together and each played his part.
- He monitored the process and evaluated the result – they gathered 12 basketsful of left-overs and knew how many they had fed.

Some or all of these 'cross-cutting' skills are essential for all types of successful transformational development. They provide support to the programme and help maintain focus and direction. It is impossible to determine accurately the end from the beginning, but thorough planning and monitoring will help keep the anticipated end-point in view and determine when mid-course adjustments need to be made.

Good Practice in cross-cutting issues helps maintain focus and contributes to ensuring a successful and sustainable outcome.

The Church

One specific 'cross-cutting' or contextual issue is the governmental relationship between the practitioners involved in a social action activity and the Church. As a family of churches in *Newfrontiers* we believe strongly that the biblical vehicle for change (i.e. the 'change agent') is the Church. Social action projects often arise from an individual with vision and passion who will give '200%' energy to bring about change and serve those who are in some way disadvantaged. Such individuals have a tendency to have tunnel vision and be highly focused; they find it hard to understand why the rest of the world does not feel as passionately about an issue as they do; their temptation is to 'go for it' regardless of what else is happening. This is the very place where the church elders have an essential role. Sadly, situations abound where individuals have acted independently and ended up with, at best, ineffectual ministries and, at worst, chaos and disaster, sometimes including their own burnout.

What is the role of eldership? Under apostolic oversight they are charged with the care and discipleship of their people. As such, the ministries of the Church, and those who serve in them, must come within the governmental orbit of their responsibilities. These responsibilities include:

- Ensuring that the particular ministry conforms to the vision of the church.
- Ensuring that those serving in the ministry are genuinely operating under the oversight of the elders, not independently – regular meetings for prayer and discussion are essential.
- Encouraging those who serve to be equipped through training, etc. – the elders do not, of course, have to provide this 'skills' training themselves.
- Supporting and caring for those ministering, for example to protect them against 'burnout'.

The Church is God's instrument for our security. To by-pass the elders and act independently falls well short of God's best for us and those we are seeking to serve. Additionally, it is important for the membership of the church to be aware of and to participate in the vision and activities as far as is practicable. Openness and good communication will both heighten the level of active participation and also broaden the support base of prayer and financial giving.

*Good Practice is to work out of the local church under
the spiritual authority of the local eldership.*

2.3 Practice

In day-to-day terms, ministry to poor people often begins with some specific practice – the provision, say, of water or food, shelter or clothing. In such activity the heart of Jesus is apparent. He looked on the people and saw them as 'sheep without a shepherd' (Mk 6:34). He allowed this to deflect him from his previously determined course (to go aside with his disciples) and he responded out of compassion and love. May we never lose such a willingness to 'break the rules' as the Spirit leads and to be people of compassion!

Recently, God spoke prophetically[46] that he would raise up 'Champions of Compassion'. I can envisage a day when there is such a champion in every apostolic sphere to help implement and fulfil the apostolic commission to remember the poor.

In what areas of practice might we expect to be active? These may fall into two categories: 1) those related to a specific sector or theme (e.g. health, agriculture, HIV, literacy) and 2) those related to a particular people group (e.g. street children, elderly people). There is sometimes a blurred line between these but for the present illustration precision is not essential.

Here are just a few examples – the list is far from exhaustive:

Sector / Theme	People group

• Water/sanitation
• Agriculture
• Education
  Formal
  Informal
• Health
  Clinics
  HIV/AIDS
  Leprosy
• Income generation
  Micro-enterprise
  Business start up
• Advocacy for
  individuals – not
  'issues'
	• Children
	  Street
	  OVCs
	• Asylum seekers
	• Elderly people
	• Women
	  Abuse
	  Sex trade
	  Crisis pregnancy
	• Prisoners

[46]This prophetic word was given in the context of a gathering of men with apostolic and prophetic gifting from around the world.

These are, of course, areas and people groups which have attracted much attention from both Christian and secular workers over the years. Much material exists which relates to good practice and which describes what others have found works successfully. We must be careful not to reinvent the wheel but to build on Good Practice where it exists, remembering that what works in one setting may not be readily transferable to another. Principles rather than specific practice are probably the key issues on which we should concentrate.

Much Good Practice material exists to describe what others have found works successfully.

Principles rather than specific practice are probably the key issues on which we should concentrate.

3. Key Indicators of Good Practice

3.1 What are Good Practice Indicators?

There is a general recognition that certain ministries are excellent, such as the Foundations for Farming initiative in Zimbabwe where traditional yields of 250kg per hectare have been multiplied ten-fold, or more. But what are the features we are seeing that allow us to come to such a conclusion? Definition of why this judgement can be made may be by quantifying, for instance, 'before and after' statistics of yields in terms of tonnes per hectare. In other contexts we may count the number of churches planted or individuals saved, or record the beneficial effects in peoples' lives, such as children being able to attend school.

However, not all community development activity can be assessed in this way. When is a clinic considered to be successful? Or what about a street children's project?

Measurements of some aspects may be possible, but there would also be less tangible qualities which might indicate excellence. These may be more intuitive than measured, but nevertheless would still be valid.

Through identifying Key Indicators we are seeking to highlight characteristics which most would agree are integral to an excellent ministry. Not all would be present in every ministry but the majority will be evident.

3.2 *How can these Key Indicators be used?*

No list of indicators can be exhaustive but we will consider 20 which have been demonstrated to be of value. There are two ways in which we believe that these indicators are helpful. First, where churches are planning a particular ministry these indicators provide a useful checklist of both values and practice. The list is not exhaustive and as you plan there may be others that occur to you. However, it provides a good starting point.

The second way in which they can be useful is in monitoring performance once the ministry is active. By considering each indicator in turn you can ask yourself first whether it is true for that ministry and then reflect on how you can improve in that particular area. Objective monitoring and evaluation should be a priority and this list provides some 'pegs' on which this process can be hung. (A Ministry Health Check using this material is described on my website www.NigelRing.org)

3.3 *Categories*

The indicators are presented in two groups. Group A includes matters related to integration of the ministry within the local church, leadership and the spiritual impact the ministry can make. Group B relates to skills which may be specific to the ministry or which would apply to all ministries, e.g. handling finance.

Group A: Church and leadership issues
In this category the following issues are identified:
- Apostolic endorsement;
- Local church eldership oversight;
- Hearing God;
- Vision to be clear;
- Gospel impact;
- Individuals changed from poverty to active mission;
- Kingdom extension to be intentional;
- Biblical principles to be clearly defined.

A1   Apostolically endorsed
When writing to the Gentile church in Galatia, Paul told them of his commission from the apostles in Jerusalem to take the gospel to the Gentiles. Their only injunction was that he should 'remember the poor' which was 'the very thing he was eager to do' (Gal 2:10).

Although this refers to the poor among the believers, it illustrates the apostolic mandate that the poor should be major beneficiaries of the fruit of the gospel, as prophesied in the 'Kingdom manifesto' that we should 'bring good news to the poor' (Is 61:1–3). The ministry has the support and backing of the apostolic oversight.

Apostolic ministry is part of God's 'plan A' (there is no biblical plan B!) to assist local leadership to bring their people to maturity (Eph 4:12–16). Accordingly, it is vital that ministry embracing the poor within the local church should have clear apostolic endorsement and confirmation that the vision is appropriate to the overall vision of the church.

A2   Local church eldership oversight
Elders are the anointed leaders of the local church. They are

responsible for the spiritual welfare of the believers in their care and will, one day, stand before God's judgement seat to give account for each one. They do not have a priestly function between God and the believers but they do have a fathering and caring responsibility to bring each of the believers to maturity.

Frequently those with a passion to help the poor are 'tunnel-visioned', with an intense focus on the ministry they believe God has called them to. Often they are very self-sacrificial of their time and material possessions, and can feel a frustration that others are not as passionate as they are. This can lead to independence – often with disastrous results.

God's primary vehicle for advancing the Kingdom is the local church. It is essential that ministries with the poor enjoy the genuine and active oversight of the elders. This brings security to those involved and fruitfulness that comes out of walking in a godly way. It also ensures that the ministry is intimately knit into the vision and life of the local church, not acting as a self-contained activity.

A3 Hearing God

Jesus did nothing on his own initiative but always did the things that pleased the Father (Jn 8:28, 29).

It is vital that we are clear that we are in the centre of God's will in whatever ministry we undertake, not only because we are called to be obedient to him but also because, when the going gets tough (and it will!), we need to be able to have the confidence that we are on-track with him and are not just following a good idea. We must have the certainty that God has spoken and commissioned the ministry.

A4 Vision to be clear

'Where there is no vision, the people are unrestrained' (Prov 29:18, NASB).

If we lack vision we have no clearly defined track to travel on, our destination is uncertain. For any ministry to be successful there must be a sense of purpose and direction for what is being implemented, with agreed goals, objectives and expectations (see B1 Project Cycle Management below). A vision may change or grow (one translation of the above verse uses 'progressive vision') and need not be seen as 'cast in concrete'. Nevertheless, its clear definition at all stages provides a framework and spur to faith.

A5 Gospel impact

The Kingdom mandate of Isaiah 61 shows how, in the space of three verses, the poor can be lifted from abject poverty to active mission. Preaching good news helps people to become 'oaks of righteousness, the planting of the Lord'. There are then examples of how this is demonstrated through increased influence and reputation even across the nations (Is 61:4–9).

Successful ministry with the poor should have the clear expectation that lives will not be just 'patched up' with people being lifted out of poverty to a better lifestyle, important as that is. There should be an eternal dimension which they are exposed to, for only the gospel can bring about the heart transformation that will truly lift people into a place of hope and fruitfulness. So, there should be clear goals and expectations that gospel fruit will be evident in people's lives. The gospel should be at the heart of all that we do – what some call 'integral mission'.

A6 Individuals changed from poverty to active mission

One goal of the ministry should be to move people from poverty (spiritual and material) to fruitfulness in the mission of the church (redemptive lift). The gospel has to be good news for all and one of the benefits that can be expected is to lift people from requiring ongoing support to becoming contributors to their local community and participators in the mission of the church.

A7 Kingdom extension to be intentional

Ministry with the poor provides a fertile context for God's rule and government to be made manifest. People who already recognise their weakness and need of help are often more receptive to the gospel than those who are surrounded with apparent material security.

Through ministry with the poor there should be a clear expectation that the Kingdom of God will be extended in defined ways, e.g. through church planting, challenging injustice and sharing the gospel.

A8 Biblical principles to be clearly defined

The Church should be exemplary in all its dealings. The Bible has much to say about righteousness, mercy and love. Such expressions of godliness should cause the world to take note. A conspicuous contrast with the world should be seen in our stewardship, compassion, faith, wisdom etc.

Group B: Ministry-related matters

In this category the following issues are identified:
- Project Cycle Management;
- Finance;
- Mature leadership;
- Responding to gifting / passion;
- Pastoral support;
- Training;
- Impact;
- Partnering / networking;
- Local community ownership;
- Sustainability;

- Scaling up and multiplication;
- Use of God-given resources.

B1 Project Cycle Management

Project Cycle Management is a powerful tool for planning, implementing and evaluating a project or ministry to ensure a successful outcome. It helps us answer such questions as:

- Where are we now?
- Where are we going?
- How are we going to get there?
- How are we going to know we have arrived?

There are four key components in the process:

a) Identification of what the project will focus on – a needs assessment is a helpful tool to achieve this.

b) Planning and design of the project including clearly defined objectives, timeline and budget.

c) Monitoring at regular intervals to ensure that the anticipated programme is being followed. This allows for adjustments to be made if external conditions or other matters are likely to affect the achievement of the goals, or delays are inevitable.

d) Evaluation. This is carried out at the end of the project, or after each significant stage, in order to review the extent to which the intended outcomes have been accomplished and to define the lessons which may be learned both for the benefit of future projects within the church and elsewhere.

Project Cycle Management is a very powerful and effective tool but a full treatment of the techniques involved is beyond the scope of this book. You are encouraged to read further, e.g. Book 5 in Tearfund's excellent series 'Roots' available on line in various languages:

http://tilz.tearfund.org/webdocs/Tilz/Roots/English/PCM/PCM_E.pdf

B2 *Finance*

Finance is the one thing most likely to cause ship-wreck to a ministry. Much could be said but the two most important features to consider are *stewardship* and *transparency*.

Stewardship is about faithfulness – ensuring that funds are used effectively and that donor funds are 'ring fenced' and not used for purposes other than that for which they were given.

Transparency and accountability recognise that money is the devil's playground and accountability is our safeguard. This requires basic elements of 'good practice' such as:

- project planning / budgeting to avoid having to ask for more because an activity over-runs the estimated cost;
- good record-keeping to maintain a 'trail' for every transaction;
- accountability to the donor to demonstrate that the funds have been used for the intended purpose.

B3 *Mature leadership*

Ministry which embraces the poor can be very demanding. Often activists are in hostile environments, either due to the types of people being reached or to the secular context in which they are operating. Leaders of a project should be spiritually mature both for their own health and for the sake of those they are leading.

B4 *Responding to gifting / passion*

In Exodus 31 and 35, in which the construction of the tabernacle is being described, there are frequent references to the workers' skills as they apply their particular gifting to the work, such as spinning goats' hair, or donating wealth, jewellery or other materials. We also read of their heart attitude, e.g. everyone 'whose heart moved him' (Ex 35:21,

22, 26). When defining a ministry it should ideally combine the need for such a ministry with the availability of people's gifting and according to their passion. The workers are chosen and involved because of a personal sense of call and because they are appropriately gifted. The result of having such a team will be great commitment and diligence. It also gives reason why those particular individuals are available within the Church – God has provided them for such a purpose.

B5 *Pastoral support*

Workers are frequently in the front line of opposition. They may see and experience much ungodliness and opposition, so it is important that they have appropriate oversight, good pastoral support and encouragement. As discussed in section 2.1, pastoral support is essential. Sharing the burden of the ministry can restore a distorted interpretation of a situation to a more balanced perspective. A safe environment in which people can 'off-load' is vital. Even with less demanding ministries it is important for people to feel supported and directed, which is the practice of good management.

B6 *Training*

Training is important for several reasons. First, people should feel they are providing the 'best practice' that is known, and so training in the necessary 'hands on' skills is empowering. Second, training in more peripheral matters leads to greater fulfilment and satisfaction. Third, the process of 'training trainers' allows preparation and provision to be made for the future multiplication of the ministry. All members of the team should regularly be given appropriate training.

B7 Impact

When the ministry is planned, clear goals and expectations need to be defined (see A4 Vision and B1 Project Cycle Management, above). The processes of monitoring and evaluating reveal whether the ministry is accomplishing the goals which were identified at the start and whether the intended impact is being achieved for the beneficiaries.

B8 Partnering / networking

Steps are taken to liaise with other groups in order to strengthen the activities either through active partnership or through networking. Too often people work in isolation and deny themselves much good experience that others have acquired. Partnership implies a working relationship either in the ministry or through funding, whereas a network tends to be more informal. Its success depends on the willingness of all parties to share knowledge and support one another as may be appropriate. A more formally defined network can also be valuable for providing a resource of knowledge and experience to others who may be considering setting up an equivalent ministry or in need of assistance.

B9 Local community ownership

Some ministries are contained within the local church whereas others intentionally impact a local community. Where this is the case, the active co-operation of the local community may represent one key to success. Often the community will have a better understanding of the culture you may be trying to impact than is readily available within the local church. The ministry should be as integrated as possible within the local community, with active participation in its planning and execution, provided this can be achieved without compromising the Christian values of spiritual leadership.

B10 *Sustainability*

Donor dependency both represents a vulnerability for a ministry, in that there is no guarantee of ongoing funding, and also imposes a lack of dignity. A thorough assessment should be made and practice implemented to make the ministry as self-sustainable as possible so that it is locally 'owned' and not donor-dependent. Nevertheless, certain ministries are inherently unable to become financially independent. This may require exploring 'special relationships' with locally based donors or with other churches who may have a relational commitment, rather than depending on the need for sustained fund-raising.

B11 *Scaling up and multiplication*

Although some ministries have clearly defined and appropriate boundaries, most have the potential either to grow and multiply, or to be reproduced in other settings where appropriate, bearing in mind the importance of sensitivity to context. For instance, it may be appropriate for one ministry to 'give birth' to a similar ministry in another part of a city. An awareness of such a possibility should encourage the ministry to keep careful records about its progress (which will anyway help with monitoring) and seek networking contacts.

B12 *Use of God-given resources*

Through 'Appreciative Inquiry' people can be taught to find solutions to their difficulties by observing and mobilising the resources around them and by recognising what they have within themselves. They thus become contributors to the solution rather than just 'receivers' (2 Cor 8:3–5). Great fulfilment comes to someone who has succeeded in using their local context and sphere of influence to make a positive contribution to their welfare.

Conclusion

When God looked on his creation and declared it 'good' he was also making a statement about his own character – perfection. As we, who are made in God's image, seek to pursue excellence we can be confident that we shall be touching his heart and will one day hear the commendation, 'well done, good and faithful servant'.

In this chapter we have considered various elements that will help us to achieve such a commendation (not that our acceptance by him is dependent on what we have done!). By considering people, process and practice we have defined some principles of Good Practice. Then, through the section on Key Indicators, we have brought practical application to these principles.

Chapter 7
Some practicalities

A biblical model for caring for the needy in a local church community

Steven Oliver and Alan Norton

One evening in 1997, I faced a real dilemma. The following day I was meeting with a group of leaders from Dihlabeng Church (in South Africa's rural eastern Free State) in order to find a solution for how we were going to take care of the many widows and children suffering in our church community. The situation seemed so much bigger and more complex than I felt we could manage. However, faced with this significant challenge, I made a discovery that changed my thinking! I discovered 1 Timothy 5:3–16. This passage of Scripture is part of a letter from a wise apostle to his young apostolic delegate instructing him how to care for the widows and orphans in the Ephesian church community. It was like discovering a large gold deposit!

Inspired by the Spirit, we unlocked some of the principles of serving and empowering the poor, which we still use today. Paul is so detailed and helpful in the way he instructs his young counterpart. Here are some of the principles we discovered:

- Care should be provided for those who are 'really in need' (1 Tim 5:3); consequently, it is important to identify those who are really in need, to discern their particular need.

- The widow's family is firstly responsible (1 Tim 5:4,8); therefore the church community should not take on responsibility where there are family members who should rather be encouraged and assisted to take up the responsibility to care for the widow themselves.
- Those in need have to be practising good spiritual disciplines (1 Tim 5:5); they should pray night and day, continually putting their hope in God and looking for his intervention and help.
- They have to be living a life pleasing to God rather than living to please themselves (1 Tim 5:6); Ephesians 5:10 exhorts everyone to 'find out what pleases the Lord'.
- They must be fully participating in the local church community, humbly serving others, faithfully helping those in trouble, showing hospitality and devoting themselves to all kinds of good deeds (1 Tim 5:10).
- They should not be idle and given to gossip (1 Tim 5:13); 2 Thessalonians 3:10 teaches that 'if a man will not work, he shall not eat'.

In essence, what we learnt from this passage of Scripture guided us as a community at Dihlabeng Church in how we would respond to the poor among us who had an identifiable need. We stressed to the needy at the outset that we would be working together with them in a genuine partnership. They would be as responsible for success as the church community. In this partnership the church community undertook the following:

- To assist where possible in restoring the needy person's family network to ensure appropriate provision within the family;
- To provide food and basic necessities for a limited

period to supplement whatever was already available in order to meet the immediate crisis;

- To help equip the needy person to become employable, and together to find a way that they could provide for their needs on an ongoing basis.

In addition, it was agreed that a monthly visit would be scheduled to the person in need in order to encourage them as they looked to God, and to mentor and equip them.

Armed with the principles found in 1 Timothy 5, we began in Clarens what has become a really effective work among the poor, encompassing education, skills empowerment, care of vulnerable children, care for the elderly, advocacy, care for HIV/AIDS sufferers and job creation. Such has been the impact of this local church in Clarens that the region surrounding the town, which includes an area comprising five towns, took the name of the church in 2004 – Dihlabeng.

The Church and non-governmental organisations

Alan Norton

As Christians, we work in the world, but are not of it. We are called and set apart, yet we live and work within society and under rulers, governors and authorities. What should the relationship of the Church be to the world? Is the Church the same as a non-governmental organisation (NGO)? Can the Church be an NGO? What are the biblical principles that inform our responses to these questions? Are there particular dangers associated with being an NGO, and how can we anticipate them?

In attempting to answer these questions, I shall relate something of our own story and experiences as a church community in Zimbabwe, and then look at some of the biblical principles to be considered and lessons learnt from experience.

Our story

River of Life Westgate Church was planted into a peri-urban area on the outskirts of Harare, Zimbabwe in 2002. The local population is characterised by high unemployment (about 75% in 2007), poverty and the devastating effects of HIV/AIDS on the lives of the people. The church immediately started to respond to these needs and various ministries were born that addressed home-based care, health, street children and education.

In addition, the church took over 'Operation Joseph', a country-wide ministry promoting Foundations for Farming, a form of sustainable farming that teaches biblical principles applicable to much of life, and reaching at the time 2500 families but subsequently expanded to 9600 families. Cedar Family Care was initiated, a ministry that responds to people infected and affected by HIV/AIDS (widows, orphans and vulnerable children) and active at 65 of the 82 'Operation Joseph' sites, reaching over 4500 families.

Work into the local community requires people and patients to come to the church premises as well as staff to be active in the community and visiting peoples' homes. The country-wide ministries require site visits by our staff at least four times per year as well as volunteers from these sites to travel into Harare for training and equipping. Some of the sites are in the remotest areas of Zimbabwe, requiring several hours of travel to get there. There are also other organisations addressing these needs both locally and around the country, as well as the Government who have their own programmes addressing the various needs.

Recognising that we needed to have some form of formal recognition and operational covering, we applied early in 2002 for Private Voluntary Organisation (PVO) status through the local Government Department of Social Welfare, which effectively meant that we would be registered as an NGO. Initially we followed up regularly on the application, with many unfulfilled promises being made but no registration forthcoming. Months turned into years and in time we realised that as the church we were enjoying much favour without PVO registration, for we had unrestricted access to rural areas and were not treated with suspicion as NGOs often were. Indeed, it appeared that being a registered NGO put one in the spotlight of suspicion, a situation that made work into rural communities much more complicated. Thus we stopped chasing our PVO application, feeling it was not in our interests to draw attention to ourselves in a fairly sensitive political and economic environment.

Late in 2006 we heard via the grapevine that our application had been approved and because we were starting to experience operating difficulties at a few of our sites in the rural areas, we eventually collected the PVO certificate. The registration had in fact been approved in 2004! Subsequently we sent in our first reports (narrative and financial) covering the period 2004 to 2006. We then engaged in more formal talks with local government officials at some of the sites so as to build relationship and clear any suspicions that may have arisen regarding our activities.

In 2007 increasing sensitivity by the ruling party about the activities of NGOs meant that we were having to use our official NGO status more and more to facilitate our operating in various rural areas. This caused some delays, but overall we were able to continue our operations in all areas despite the political tensions that were running high in the approach to the general election of 2008.

Over the years our involvement with humanitarian work has meant that we attend regular meetings with other NGOs (most of whom are not Christian). These meetings have been a tremendous help towards understanding the situation, co-ordinating and reducing overlap of efforts, and learning new ideas and approaches to relief and development work.

Lessons learnt and some relevant biblical principles

Jesus said, 'I will build my church...' (Matt 16:18). The Church is the Church and at no point should she exchange her status in order to become an NGO. Christ died for her and it is for her that he will one day return, when the wedding of the bride (Church) and groom (Jesus) will take place. In our case we registered as an NGO, but only to comply with the requirements of the governing authority and because it was prudent to do so. Jesus himself calls us to be as wise as serpents and as gentle as doves. However, the Church is not an NGO!

At the heart of everything that we do as Church is humanity's need to be saved, reconciled to God. This should be the ultimate goal of all our efforts whether we are free to operate as the Church or have to work under the cover of being an NGO. The gospel must be central to our work among the poor.

Over the years at various stages we have been encouraged to separate out the 'projects' from the 'church' per se, so as to protect the church and allow for greater autonomy in the various activities, and to enable other organisations to join without being threatened by the local church. There appears to be some good logic and reasoning to this, but each time we have been fully convinced from

Scripture that what we are doing is Church, that the 'projects' are essentially ministries of the Church, and that their rightful place is within the authority and vision of the local church eldership. Were we to move these ministries or projects out of the church, we would create 'para-church' and lose the power of the local church at work. Having said this, we also see the place for apostolic ministries that span a number of different local churches, providing apostolic guidance and input to them. However, those who work on the projects are to be full members of their local church with accountability to and oversight from both the ministry and their local church. We would not deploy 'lone ranger' Christians who are not fully integrated into their local church.

Romans 13:1–5 exhorts us to submit to the governing authorities since they are established by God himself; rebelling against the governing authorities is rebelling against what God has instituted, and rulers indeed hold terror for those who do wrong. Governments are there to rule, administer, govern and thus will want to know what organisations (including NGOs) are doing. In our case, this has meant that we were obliged to obtain PVO (NGO) registration in order to comply with some of the government's requirements to operate in rural areas. However, with regard to other matters and in other contexts there may be greater freedom to determine the action one takes; here one needs to be wise and interpret the times and seasons carefully. Different approaches may be particularly appropriate for different times and circumstances, as we have found in seeking to respond to the changing circumstances within Zimbabwe.

The Church will enjoy a different status depending on which country one is in. In Zimbabwe our experience has been that the Church enjoys much respect and freedom. But in other countries there may be little freedom for the Church to operate. Having established what the attitudes are of the particular governing authorities to the Church, one can determine how the Church should operate. In some situations operating as an NGO may be the most effective way for the Church to operate.

From our experience it is best to build relationships with governing officials early on rather than have to fight fires after misunderstandings have arisen about what we do or after suspicions have been aroused. In many cases we have enjoyed much support from government officials.

NGO status invariably means meeting and mixing with other agencies and NGO staff, many of whom are not Christian. It is a wonderful opportunity to be salt and light! However, we always need to be on our guard, aware that there is an enemy prowling around like a roaring lion, seeking whom he may devour and looking for every opportunity to undermine or sink our good efforts. At NGO meetings we hear ideas that are very logical, make sense, are reasonable and may even have Christian principles in the mix. However, we need to watch out! We are called to far more than what is logical, makes good sense, or is seen by the world as best practice. Instead we are called to obey God, whose ways are not our ways. These ways may sometimes appear as foolishness and bring us into conflict with the world. Therefore we are to seek God and demonstrate our love for him through obedience. Test and filter everything by the Word and Spirit.

For this reason James warns us that pure and faultless religion is not only caring for widows and orphans in their distress but also 'to keep oneself from being polluted by the world' (Jas 1:27). This pollution is often a gradual and subtle thing and therefore something to be conscious of in the context of engaging in regular meetings with the institutions of this world. We are also warned not to be unequally yoked with unbelievers (2 Cor 6:14). Therefore do not make treaties or get yoked to unbelieving NGOs. Rather, we are to serve as Jesus taught and demonstrated.

In summary, let the Church be the Church as far as is permissible and is wise in the operating environment, yet meanwhile submitting to the governing authorities and using local legislation prudently for the extension of the Kingdom of God.

Chapter 8

Lives transformed

Nigel Ring

In this book we have been considering the theology of the poor and have been looking at some practical responses to ensure this theology is firmly rooted in reality. We have seen how God's heart is not just to see those who are poor and disadvantaged being given a 'hand up'. His heart is to see them reach the full potential he purposed for them from before the foundation of the world and for them to be released into active mission within his Kingdom purposes.

With this in mind it seems appropriate to close this book with some real-life stories about people who have successfully walked this path and are now living in the freedom God intended. As you read these stories we encourage you to try to get inside them and see life through the eyes of those who are sharing, engaging with the challenges they faced, and then rejoicing with them in the liberty and fulfilment they are now experiencing by living in the centre of God's will. That is the place he intends for each one of us. It is our prayer that through reading these testimonies you will put this book down not merely having been informed but that they will cause you to be drawn closer to God in worship of the One who is able to bring about life-changing transformation. May he receive all the glory!

Justice's story

From the ash heap, to be with the princes of his people

Gavin Northcote[47]
South Africa

'My name is Justice. I have come to be saved.' These words are etched in my memory of the planting of Dihlabeng Church on Kromdraai Farm near Clarens, South Africa in November 1996. They were spoken by Justice Mofokeng as he introduced himself to Steven Oliver, a week after the initial church meeting in the barn on Steven's farm. The gospel had come to him in a place which had previously harboured terrifying memories of oppression and hatred; but now it was a place of joy and celebration of God's grace and favour, and Justice's life would never be the same again.

Justice was born on Kromdraai Farm in 1964, the youngest of nine children. His parents were poor farm labourers, living with their family in a small village. In keeping with the practices of apartheid, the village was fenced off from the rest of the farm and the children lived in fear of punishment from the farmer should they stray from the confines of the village. They were restricted and bound not only in their movements, but also in the African traditional religion of worshipping their ancestors. This meant that they continually had to pay homage to their deceased relatives, particularly parents and grandparents. They lived in constant fear of the severe consequences of not satisfying the apparent demands of their ancestors. These demands would be communicated through witchdoctors called *sangomas*.

---

[47]Gavin Northcote serves as a fellow elder with Justice Mofokeng at Dihlabeng Church in Clarens, South Africa.

Justice's family was expelled from their home on the farm in 1980, and his father took the family across the Caledon River which forms both the eastern boundary of Kromdraai and the border with Lesotho. This move caused them immense suffering and hardship as they moved from one state of abject poverty to another. Lesotho is one of the poorest nations globally. In spite of this great hardship, Justice completed his schooling and was contemplating a career in the Police, when he started to have dreams about preaching the Word of God. In these dreams a man spoke to him, telling him that he would do no work other than preaching the gospel. Because of his family's ignorance and superstitions, they were afraid of these dreams and tried to persuade him not to dwell on them. But the dreams persisted, until the day that Steven and Heather Oliver and their family arrived on Kromdraai Farm in July 1996, the place where Justice was born 32 years previously.

News soon spread from farm to farm and village to village that a church meeting was going to be held on the first Sunday in November. At the first meeting, over 500 people gathered, some having crossed the Caledon River from Lesotho to attend, and sixty-four people were saved that day. Although Justice attended that first meeting, he was not among those who were saved. He was once more on the farm which brought back childhood memories of oppression and suffering. What he now saw and heard in the barn was the sound of exuberant celebration and of people praising God. A preacher was sharing the good news that Jesus Christ had come to earth to die on a cross for our sin, that whosoever would believe in him would be saved. He was terrified and did not respond to the gospel that day.

Throughout the following week, he began to feel God calling him to repentance and to surrender his life to Christ. All the dreams he had been having over the years were starting to make sense. His family continued to press him to forget the dream, but Justice could not resist the gospel call. Such was the urgency of what he was feeling that before the meeting started the next Sunday, Justice introduced himself to Steven and declared, 'I have come to be saved'. At the end of the meeting, when Steven asked people to respond to the good news that Jesus had died for their sins, Justice walked forward. Little did he know that Steve had received a promise from God that he would hand-pick the leaders to help him in this great work; here was the first of many.

While Justice was savouring the joy of being a new creation, and experiencing wonderful acceptance and love from those around him, he was again challenged by the fears of the past as Steven invited him into his home to sit at his table and enjoy lunch together. To have a white South African man invite him into his house to eat and talk was a new experience and a moment he will never forget. This was the house from where suffering and injury had been inflicted upon him and his family, and now God was demolishing the dividing walls of mistrust, suspicion, racism and hatred as they ate around the table that day.

Justice's growth, as a Christian and as a leader, took shape in the weeks and months which followed. Being a man of just over six feet in height, one would have expected that he was well respected and had aspirations of leadership among his people in Lesotho. But this was not the case. He despised who he was, and thought of his life as being insignificant, all reinforced by his poverty. The gospel now came and changed all that, restoring his dignity by showing him his value in becoming a child of God. His wife and children came to salvation as well as his parents, brothers and sisters. He was baptised in the Holy Spirit along with a small group of leaders Steven had been gathering weekly for teaching and prayer. Justice soon became Steven's right hand man and translator among the Sesotho-speaking people, and together they preached the gospel every Sunday at Kromdraai. The fire of an evangelist burned inside him as, week after week in the barn, he saw many people saved, strongholds of witchcraft and ancestral worship demolished, and people set free. At the frequent funerals which Justice attended in Lesotho and on the surrounding South African farms, traditional Basotho practices of ancestral worship at the graveside were replaced with the message of the gospel as he began to seize every opportunity to preach, and many people were saved and added to Dihlabeng Church in this way. With Steven being ignorant of the Basotho cultural practices and norms in the early years of the church, he relied on Justice to guide him through some very tricky cultural minefields and blunders.

Steven asked Justice to join him on the staff of Dihlabeng Church. Justice and his wife, Anna, were able to move their three daughters to South Africa to be closer to the church when the meeting place moved from the barn on Steven's farm to the town of Clarens. Today, Justice is inheriting many of the promises which he received from God when he was newly saved. He is an elder in Dihlabeng Church and has been part of many church planting teams into neighbouring towns such as Manyatseng in Ladybrand, and across the border into the nation of Lesotho when City of Joy Church was planted in Maseru in April 2006. Mention the words 'church plant' in his presence and he's immediately asking if he can be part of the action.

In our local community of Clarens, Justice has come to be respected and admired for his passion for the gospel, and for his day-to-day commitment to displaying the gospel's power and influence in his own life and the life of the church. At Dihlabeng Church he is loved by both rich and poor alike, and he navigates cultural differences and challenges with ease as he shepherds and cares for the flock of God.

Psalm 113:7 says that '…He raises the poor from the dust and lifts the needy from the ash heap; he seats them with princes, with the princes of their people.' Justice's life, and the story of how the gospel changed him, is surely a testimony to this promise we have from scripture. From growing up under oppressive circumstances, suffering the indignity of extreme poverty, to hearing and responding to the gospel, and enjoying the outworking of God's grace upon his life, Justice has been caught up into world mission, to take the gospel to every nation, tribe and tongue.

Anna's story

Totally transformed

Anna Omelchenko
Russia

I grew up in a loving family where life was good. I am an inquisitive and curious person by nature and I thought that I would try drugs just to see what they were like. I did not foresee any problem. I was in control and I would just sample drugs for the experience. Gradually, step by step, I took more and more until I found that l had become addicted. During this time I married a man who also was a drug addict and one day it dawned on me that I was in a terrible pit.

We attempted to start a new life and took the decision that there would be no more drugs. It was during this time that our son was born. At the time of the birth I was praying the Lord's Prayer – it was the only prayer that I knew. As I look back now, knowing what an amazing gift our son is, I realise that God must have been at work because I stayed free of drugs for two years.

Six months after the birth of our son we found ourselves being drawn back into the world of drugs. Things became as bad as they ever were. We sought help from parents, clinics, doctors and even witchcraft, but nothing helped or made any difference. We could not get free. My husband was in and out of prison at this time, and continued with the drugs when at home. We had no proper family life.

Things became very bad. At this time all I was certain of was death. I had lost my parents and my husband died; I lost all my friends and my home. My son, Vova, was being cared for by my husband's parents. He was all that I had left in the world. My body was in decline; every time I cut myself it was infected with abscesses, and my organs were breaking down. I could not speak properly and my weight had gone down to 38 kilos. No one wanted to speak to me or to have anything to do with me. As my body collapsed, I simply had no more fight left in me and death was staring me in the face.

I had a death sentence over me and those around me expected that I would not live much longer. But there were people from the church here in Armavir who knew of me because my mum attended the church and, although I did not realise it, they had started praying for me when I was on drugs. Valera Selesnev suggested that I go to the Podgornay Rehab Centre, and my brother took me to the Rehab Centre, but I was initially turned down as I was so desperately ill and so near to death.

Then a miracle happened. Even though I was so close to death, the Rehab Centre reviewed their decision and agreed to take me in. Within two weeks I felt God start to work in my life. Day by day I experienced God's presence and provision. It was the happiest time of my life. I began to understand the love and grace of God.

I spent one year at the Rehab Centre and then returned to Armavir free from drugs and healed; but this transition was a very hard and difficult time for me. No one believed that I was really free of drugs, and that I had changed and could stand on my own two feet. A period of years ensued during which it seemed as if people were simply watching and waiting for me to fall back into the old ways. But, as they observed me, they could see the real transformation that God had done in my life.

I found a job in a kindergarten; I had been trained as a teacher. The teachers there were continually asking questions of me and so I was often able to give my testimony about what God had done in my life. It was very natural for me to share in this way and all the teachers came to Christ.

Subsequently I moved to a new job with a local TV station in Armavir. The head of the TV station had decided to produce a programme about the Christian faith and he offered me the job of launching this programme, which is called 'Open Heaven'. Now that I am working there I am finding it a wonderful way of sharing the gospel with other people as we talk about their Christian faith.

My family and friends have now come to believe that I am free from drugs and that God has brought about an amazing transformation in my life. I had been on drugs for a total of 17 years, on and off, and I can look back now and see God's miraculous intervention because in my culture and environment people very seldom live this long on drugs. Many people consider it impossible to get free after being on drugs for so long, but God has gloriously set me free.

I am so grateful to God for my son, Vova. He was indeed a special gift from God, for I had been told that I could not have children. Although I did not know God at that time, I had prayed, 'Please give me a son', and Vova was the answer to that prayer. Unfortunately, when I turned back to drugs he was placed in an orphanage. But now we are together again and he is a wonderful support. We are on our own and, although it is difficult, he understands, and when there are problems he says, 'Do not worry, Mum; we will overcome.' He is a good son and truly my helper.

I heard about the Christian school in Armavir and prayed that God would open a way for him to attend. It would be difficult financially as I did not really earn enough. In order to be considered for enrolment we had to find a teacher who could give him some extra lessons since he was behind in English. A teacher was found and in the summer he managed to catch up on the three years that he had missed in English. He started at the school in year 4. It was a struggle to keep up with the school fees which were charged since it was a private school, but I kept looking to God. People would give testimony in church about how God had provided for them and so I kept praying. It was just before Christmas one year that I just could not pay the fees. I was worried and I cried out to God. When I came to the school to say that I was not going to be able to pay, I was amazed to be told, 'Did Vova not tell you we have a sponsor for you from England?' I just fell on my knees so grateful that God faithfully supplies our needs and so thankful to the teachers of that school who have become so much a part of my family.

God has totally transformed my life, and I am so glad to tell my story because it is a real testimony to the Glory of God.

Brian's story

I am a new creation

Brian Mtarwa
Zimbabwe

I was born in Inyanga, about 300km east from Harare in Zimbabwe. Inyanga is a very beautiful place with big mountains. My father was a farm worker. When I was just two years old, my parents were divorced. That was in 1976. After my parents' divorce I lived with my mother and sister, and left school in 1991 with five 'O-levels'.

I never knew there was someone called Jesus. We used to go to a Roman Catholic church once a year at Christmas time, but that was all. There were many bad influences in the environment I grew up in – street fighting, drugs, womanising, no respect for village elders. These were very normal in my neighbourhood.

When I was 17 years old I started working as a gardener. It was very hard to make a living. My employer, a white man, befriended me, and he taught me to sniff drugs. It made my life even worse than it had been, and in a search for greener pastures I decided to go to South Africa to try and make a living from arts and crafts. There things did not improve and my focus became chasing after girls. Things didn't work out for me well in South Africa and I decided to return to Zimbabwe. Though I didn't realise it then, I now believe that God was already at work.

When I returned from South Africa I was still chasing after girls, and then one day I made an approach to a particular girl. This casual contact would have a deep significance. I asked for her address and the next day I woke up early to prepare to visit the one I hoped would become my new girlfriend. I was very excited. It was a Sunday and I was shocked to discover on arriving at the address that there was a church service at that house. I gathered up my courage and decided to go in. I found a seat in the back row – the girl I had come for was seated near the front.

The preacher came up and began to preach from Matthew that heaven and earth will pass away but God's Word never will. This really touched me. For the first time in a really long time, I started crying. I knew that I desperately needed this Word that would never pass away. I knew that I needed Jesus in my life.

I went home still thinking about this, but the next Sunday I returned to give my life to Christ. I had peace in my heart, and I just knew that the old had passed and the new had come – I am a new creation! That was in October 1995. Praise God.

God began transforming my life. I started working with street children as I felt that they too desperately needed help. For seven years I worked for a project in Harare – an experience that changed my life. I would visit these children, encourage them, teach them the Word of God, and persuade them to turn from harmful ways. I saw the hand of God on them, and many were changed by him. Some of them are now in different countries making their livelihood through the arts and craft skills we taught them.

For the pasts five years I have been a youth leader at River of Life Church Westgate, in Harare. I have also become involved in a new church planting venture called Stapleford Community Church, where I am an elder in training. I praise God that I am married to a beautiful wife, Charity, and we have a handsome son, Josh. I have a business buying cattle in the rural areas to sell as beef in Harare. God has blessed me abundantly even though life is not easy for people in the current situation in Zimbabwe.

God rescued me when my life was a mess. He cleansed me and now I am a new creation!

Greg's story

The redemptive lift of the gospel

Greg Haslam
United Kingdom

I have known some degree of poverty in my life, along with the fear and shame that attend it. I have also known Christ's power to change our circumstances beyond our wildest dreams. Along the way, I've discovered there are two basic reasons for poverty, namely, because of circumstances and because of breaking God's laws – in other words, through no fault of our own, and through the foolish things we've done. These were the roots of my poverty, but both of them were dealt with by Christ.

Along with my twin sister and elder brother, I was born in the post-World War II blitz-damaged and bleak city of Liverpool. My parents' marriage was very unhappy. Money was tight, work was scarce, tensions and domestic rows a daily reality. We children were frightened, emotionally damaged, and disturbed by the conflicts at home. My mother decided to flee from my father and find whatever housing she could. They divorced soon after. I was six years old. Life was hard. Our 'new' home was a cramped and dilapidated 'slum' property in a rough district famed for its gang fights, burglaries, drunks, graffiti and vandalism. It was dingy and austere, and regularly infested with cockroaches and fleas.

It had no bathroom or inside toilet, and no heating but a single coal fire we often couldn't afford to light. We shivered in winter and slept in damp, cramped spaces – all three children in one tiny bedroom for years. Our clothes were second-hand, jumble-sale 'cast offs', ill-fitting, well-worn and out-of-date. Food was basic, holidays non-existent, toys a rare occurrence. But all three of us were bright and did well at school, even though we felt 'odd', ashamed and 'dirt-poor' alongside other kids. Mum had to clean people's floors as a single mother to supplement her meagre National Assistance.

This left me with a fear of poverty and insecurities about the future. But God saw this and had mercy on me, bringing two great school friends into my life, David and Neil. They had recently become Christians and began sharing the gospel with me. This culminated in a chance to hear evangelist Billy Graham's 1967 London Crusade broadcast at the Methodist Central Hall in Liverpool. I came to faith in Christ that night and stepped out onto Liverpool's sunlit Lime Street, and into the full joy of Christ. My life would never be the same again, for Christ has totally transformed it ever since.

I developed a love for the Bible and a hunger for truth. The call to become a pastor came when I was just 16 years old, after hearing John Stott preach through 2 Timothy at Keswick in 1969. I was gripped by the Bible and the desire to preach it. Months later this happened. Subsequently, I studied theology at Durham University, and met and married my beautiful wife Ruth, who has been the Lord's greatest gift to me ever since. I became a High School teacher, and had three sons who all came to Christ and grew up to serve him enthusiastically. The Lord kept me from repeating my father's mistakes, and my own experiences of marriage and parenthood have been gloriously happy.

In 1978 my call to Christian ministry came to a head and I pursued further study at the London Theological Seminary. I've now served as a pastor for some three decades in two churches – for 21 years at Winchester Family Church and then at Westminster Chapel, London. These have been wonderful times, full of adventure, rich blessings from God, many miracles and the joy of being used to transform people's lives. We've seen God's abundant provision for our lives. He's provided abundantly for the churches we've pastored – staff, new church buildings, missions and equipment – totalling millions of pounds! This is what I mean by the 'redemptive lift' of the gospel. What does this do in our lives?

1. **The gospel frees us from rejection, fear and shame.**
It frees us for God's ordained future plans for our lives, so that faith and hope become realities to us. True prosperity includes protection, assurance and well-being in mind, body and soul. God gives us intellectual, creative and social fulfilment in abundance!

2. **Christ reveals to us our earthly destiny and funds it!**
'Prosperity' is not a matter of what we have in the bank (for that may be little), or how many yachts, cars, houses and luxuries we possess. It's not what we have, but what we have access to! Paul said, 'My God will meet all your needs according to his glorious riches in Christ Jesus' (Phil 4:19). We've discovered that where God leads he feeds, where he guides he provides and when we're in his will he will 'foot the bill'!

3. **We come alive spiritually and hunger for reality.**
God does this by feeding us on a rich diet of divinely revealed truth. This opens up all kinds of new perspectives to our once narrow, ignorant minds. We become Spirit-filled 'culture vultures' and see everything in God's world from new perspectives now. We discover there's nothing 'secular' except sin and begin to live for God's glory in all areas of life,

making us richer than Bill Gates or the Duke of Westminster!

4. **The message of the Bible as a whole grips us.** We see God's 'Big Picture' plans for the world Christ redeemed at the cross. We find out that God is in control and works all things together for the good of those who love him (Rom 8:28). We see his hand at work in the past painful circumstances of lives and say with Joseph, 'God intended it for good' (Gen 50:20). Every situation is now 'win-win' for us!

5. **We become givers and not takers** – 'God is able to make all grace abound to you, so that in all things at all times, having all that you need, you will abound in every good work' (2 Cor 9:8), i.e. we have enough for our own emergencies and ample spare to bless others. We cease being stingy, because with God there's plenty more where that came from!

Chavandhuka's story

Nothing is impossible with God

Chavandhuka Jenitala
Zimbabwe

I was born in 1971 on Goodhope Farm on the outskirts of Harare and grew up there. My family was poor. I left school in 1990 with two 'O-levels'. Little did I realise that I would one day become a Christian. It's amazing what happened. Jesus truly is the bread of life, my redeemer. He snatched me from the fire, from death. He has shown me amazing love.

I was a drunkard. In a Shona community, when someone is a drunkard, it's not just that he drinks too much beer. One gets caught up in lots of stuff, like fighting, adultery, theft and abusive relationships. I was involved in some of these things. I used to get drunk every day. People in the community would talk about me. They would say that I was a useless good-for-nothing and a bad guy. But God can use the weak and foolish things of this world to shame the wise. I am one of them.

It was on a Saturday afternoon in 2000 that one of the bar owners talked to me about Jesus. His name was Morgan Dzenu. We were in a beerhall when he encouraged me to go to church on the Sunday at Mount Pleasant. I was completely drunk as he spoke to me, but God is amazing. He uses people in any circumstance and any place to advance his Kingdom. Morgan knew that if I were to commit my life to Christ he would be losing much business because I was one of his best customers, together with my three friends. But he was concerned about my life and not his business. When he spoke to me about Jesus I became so excited that I was not interested in drinking any more beer that day.

Something happened to me the moment I said to Morgan that I was excited about going to church the following day. I told my friends that I was going home to prepare for the next day and that I wanted to go to church. They laughed at me. They thought I must be joking or that I had run out of stories. Some even suggested that I was mentally disturbed. However, God can work miracles. Certainly I experienced a miracle. I had never left a beerhall so early. I would always leave when they closed up, but this day something was happening to me. I left the beerhall and went to tell my wife about going to church the following day. But she didn't believe me and got angry with me. She said, 'Tell me the truth about where you are going!' She suspected that I was perhaps planning to visit a girlfriend. She shouted at me and kept insisting that I tell her the truth. She was convinced that I was lying.

I woke up early that Sunday to prepare to go to church. My wife couldn't understand this, but she didn't say anything more. I was the first one to arrive at the bus stop and, as others including Morgan arrived, they were surprised to see me at the bus stop. On my arrival at the church, the warm welcome I received from many people really touched me. I felt that this was a good place to be and I gave my life to Jesus that very day.

When I arrived back home, my wife was very excited to see me among the group of people coming from church and two weeks later she also committed her life to Jesus. I was eager to see my friends and tell them about Jesus, but they just could not believe what had happened to me. That same day I told them that I was going to drink my last beer (scud) with them. I didn't enjoy it. They thought it was going to be a temporary thing for me. After about two months Dennis, one of my friends, gave his life to Jesus. He is now a deacon in our church. The following Sunday another friend of mine, Fanuel, gave his life to Christ and he is now a house group leader in our church. Soon afterwards Morgan closed his beerhall and he too is now a house group leader and is very happy with his decision.

God has transformed my life in many ways. I am now one of the elders in our church, River of Life Westgate, here in Harare. I also own my own businesses. I run a metal-craft business that manufactures chairs, bunk beds, soil testing trays and other products. I also run a transport business and I have two seven-tonne trucks. Recently I purchased a 66-seater Scania bus which is transporting people between the city centre and Dzivarasekwa high-density suburb; and I also own three small vehicles. I am leasing a farm in Doma, which has this year produced a yield of 15 tonnes of maize, despite it having been a difficult year for agriculture. I praise God for what he has done.

This is what our God is like. He has lifted me from a place of poverty and has granted me recognition in the community. I have three children, and I also look after some orphans at my house – four of them. I am able to pay school fees for two of my late sister's children. My business supports my family and other relatives and friends as well. Nothing is impossible with God.

Christina's story

Jesus alone can set one free

Christina Buchneva
Russia

I became a Christian in 2000. At the time I had one child and was expecting another. Before that, my husband and I had been part of a gang that people were very afraid of. Everyone who knew us knew of our connections to the gang, and so people were also afraid of us. We were dealing in drugs as well as using them. My husband had had a drug and alcohol addiction for 15 years.

Because of his addictions he was stealing from our house and anywhere else he could to get money for drugs and alcohol. One day I came home to find that he had stolen virtually everything from the house. I opened the garage and the car had no wheels or engine. I just cried out, 'God help us!'

My husband became severely ill with cirrhosis of the liver. He also had hepatitis A, B & C. He had tried many different ways to get free of his addictions including doctors, witch doctors and alternative medicine, but nothing had worked. He was told it was likely that he would get only one more chance to kick his addictions, or he would die.

During this time I began praying to God, even though I didn't really believe in him. I prayed that God would either take my husband or heal him and bring him to a place of repentance. By this time our daughter was experiencing the terrible effects of these addictions.

The first time that I'd heard about God was in 1991, but as I could not give up smoking I felt there was no place for me in the church. In 1998 I saw an advert about the Rehab

Centre that the church ran and so came back to the church to ask about it. I met Volodia, and when he met with my husband there was a real joining of hearts. Volodia just made us feel so loved and accepted. Things were becoming worse and worse for us, and it began to dawn on us that God was the only way. So we came to the point of repenting and committed our lives to him.

As I was expecting my second child, I was told that this one too would have symptoms related to drug and alcohol abuse. So we started praying and were amazed to see the way that God was working in our lives. Our son was born with no ill-effects from our life of drug and alcohol abuse. We went to the Rehab Centre and after six months felt that we wanted to help other drug addicts. This is how the Mercy Mission was started in our church.

My husband and I are both now serving God in the Mercy Ministry. We oversee a safe house for children while their individual situations are dealt with by the authorities. There are 42 children there now. This provides wonderful opportunities to share what God has done in our lives, and to pass on the message that only Jesus can set us free.

We now have four children of our own. No one is frightened of us anymore, and we have just celebrated our fifth wedding anniversary. We praise God that every day now seems better than the day before. I am so grateful that God responded to my desperate cries for help at a time when I did not know him, and that he intervened and changed our lives and circumstances. He has shown that he cares for us in an amazing way.

References

Here are the bibliographical details for the printed sources that are cited in the text. Unless otherwise indicated, Bible references are from the *New International Version* (1978).

Alcorn, Randy — *Money, Possessions and Eternity* (1989) Tyndale House Publishers; Wheaton, Illinois

Atkinson, D.J. & Field, D.H. (ed.) — *New Dictionary of Christian Ethics and Pastoral Theology* (1995) Inter-Varsity Press; Leicester

CRUDAN — *Christian Wholistic Development* (2002) – a document produced by the Christian Rural and Urban Development Association of Nigeria.
[CRUDAN is a Christian, non-profit NGO engaged in development work in Nigeria with the aim of enabling churches to empower the poor.]

Meggitt, Justin J. — *Paul, Poverty and Survival* (1998) T & T Clark; Edinburgh

Myers, Bryant L — *Walking with the Poor* (1999) Orbis Books; Maryknoll, New York

Sider, Ronald J — *Rich Christians in an Age of Hunger* (1997) Word Publishing; Dallas

Stafford, Tim — Interview with John Stott, in *Newfrontiers Magazine* (January–March 2007) volume 3, issue 2

Stott, John — *Issues Facing Christians Today* (1990) Marshall Pickering; London

Wagner, C. Peter — *Churchquake: How the New Apostolic Reformation is shaking up the Church* (1999) Regal Books; Ventura, California

Yancey, Philip — *The Jesus I Never Knew* (1995) Zondervan; Grand Rapids

The Poor Deserve the Best

Nigel Ring

This practical book is an excellent complement to *Embracing the Poor*. The author takes the material he has written in one chapter of that book and expands it extensively to turn the material from theory to practice.

The goal of this book is to help churches, and Christian NGOs and Charities to raise the standard of ministries among people who are poor or disadvantaged. It is his belief that Christian ministry should be setting the example of good practice with this group of people.

Section 1 describes 20 Indicators of Good Practice, which could be expected to be an integral part of most Christian ministries that work with those who are poor or disadvantaged. They include matters that are peculiar to a Christian context, such as the relationship between the ministry and the local church leadership, and others that have general application, such as the handling of finance.

Section 2 looks at various aspects of planning a ministry. This section puts a Christian slant on tried and proven planning methods that are widely used in the development world. Techniques such as the Problem Tree, to help define the need, and the Logical Framework (logframe) are described with examples.

Section 3 describes the Ministry Health Check, a tool developed by the author from the Key Indicators in Section 1. The Health Check requires ministry teams to evaluate over 30 statements based on these Indicators. By determining how accurately they apply to the particular ministry this tool helps the team to evaluate the effectiveness of the ministry and to discuss where improvements could be made.

Section 4 tells the stories of 13 ministries which demonstrate good practice. They are drawn from a variety of nations and cultures and from across different development sectors such as health, education and agriculture. The reports have been constructed to highlight particular features which could help anyone who may be considering a similar ministry.

This is a *Newfrontiers* publication obtainable through Resources at www.NewfrontiersTogether.org. It can also be obtained through the author's website www.NigelRing.org